Special Publication No. 2   July 1994

PROJECT B.U.G.S.*
(*Better Understanding of the Great Six-leggers)
Level I

Written by:
Gary A. Dunn, M.S., F.R.E.S.
Director of Education

Young Entomologists' Society, Inc.
1915 Peggy Place
Lansing, MI 48910-2553
(517) 887-0499

ISBN 1-884256-13-9

Printed in the United States of America

Table of Contents

INTRODUCTION

TEACHING STRATEGIES AND METHODS

INSECT STUDY ACROSS THE CURRICULUM

INSECT STUDY LESSON PLANS

INTRODUCTION

Welcome to PROJECT B.U.G.S.

I hope that this PROJECT B.U.G.S. manual and the resources, educational materials, and expertise of the Young Entomologists' Society will help you introduce children to many new and exciting opportunities. In addition to being fun, both you and the children will learn about the important and fascinating world of insects and their role in the global ecology. Insects truly are the "little creatures that run the world." As you will see from the many examples given in this manual, the study of insects (entomology) lends itself very well to self-exploration and practical, direct observation. This "hands-on" suitability will appeal favorably to young people of all ages. Who knows, you may even help an enthusiastic child prepare for a career or lifetime hobby of insect study.

How to Use the PROJECT B.U.G.S. Manual

This manual offers many ideas to help you as an insect science instructor. These include suggestions for group lessons, extra information on techniques, possibilities for field trips and demonstrations, and a list of resources and references. This guide is designed to help you:
- Develop or enhance competency in insect study.
- Develop or enhance teaching techniques and skills.
- Integrate insect studies in many areas of the curriculum - arts, language, math, social studies, and other sciences.
- Know what resources are available to help you.
- Know how to guide young people in project selection, design, development, and implementation.
- Involve other adults as potential assistants.

Before your first lesson, you should become familiar with this manual, with the books and materials available in your school or public library, and with the resources available from the Young Entomologists' Society.

PROJECT B.U.G.S.: An Insect Education Curriculum

An effective insect education curriculum features the following:
- Provides activities and information that interest young people in the natural history of insects and their interactions with the environment, other living creatures, and people.
- Develops the intellectual tools needed for effective exploration of the natural world.
- Involves young people as directly as possible ("hands-on" and first-hand) in investigating the insect world by listening, watching, and exploring.
- Helps children realize that insect studies open the door to many other environmental projects and explorations.

Collectively, the key points listed in the lessons section of this manual form a conceptual framework for entomology youth education and constitute a core curriculum for the study of insects. The topics are arranged in a logical order, starting with the basics and moving on to more complex information that integrates the basics, finally culminating with insect interactions with other plants and animals, including humans.

What Will Children Learn Through PROJECT B.U.G.S.?

By taking part in entomology instruction and projects, children will:
- Discover why insects are important in both the natural and human worlds. They will learn about both beneficial and harmful insects, and the role that these (and other) "bugs" play in the local and global ecology.
- Develop, and help others develop, a healthy, realistic attitude towards insects. (Not all insects are bad!)
- Recognize the distinguishing characteristics of insects.
- Learn the parts of different types of insects.
- Learn about the growth patterns and developmental stages of insects (metamorphosis).
- Discover that there are many types of insects and that they are the largest and most diverse group of animals.
- Learn how to identify and classify insects into orders (and possibly families).
- Learn some of the ways insects find food, escape from their natural enemies, find mates, and communicate with each other.
- Learn about different methods and equipment used to observe, study, and collect insects.
- Learn different ways to preserve and display insect specimens.
- Discover what is involved in caring for different types of live insects.
- Learn how to develop and conduct a scientific experiment involving insects or other arthropods.
- Learn about the many types of careers related to entomology and the role of amateurs in entomology.
- Integrate insect projects with other activities such as photography, environmental education, horticulture, computers, art, communications, and more.
- Share their new knowledge and appreciation of insects with others through writing, speaking, demonstrations, and displays.

The Role of a PROJECT B.U.G.S. Instructor

One of your most important contributions will be setting a good example for the children to follow. It's no secret that children are fascinated with insects and other tiny critters. You can help them understand how wonderful these amazing creatures really are and how important they are to people. Show by your interest, enthusiasm, and attitude that children need not be fearful or squeamish at the sight of an insect. If you encounter a child with a serious aversion to insects, he/she is usually imitating previously seen adult behaviors. Sooner or later this behavior will disappear as the general enthusiasm of you and your group prevails.

Hopefully, one of the first things you realize as you prepare to teach children about insects is that you don't have to be an entomology expert to be a good insect science instructor. If you are able to create learning opportunities and access information and answers when needed, then you're all set. You'll learn the rest right along with the children. Of course, if you're already an experienced entomophile, then you can take it a step further and concentrate on creating new, innovative learning experiences.

There are many sources of help to assist you with instruction. There may be entomologists (professional and amateur), beekeepers, pest control operators, county extension staff, high school teachers, college faculty, and other interested adults in your community (or nearby). College students in entomology or biology may also be interested in helping at various times during the year. Personnel at county, state and federal health, agriculture, natural resource, and environmental agencies may also have training in or an interest in insects. Of course the Young Entomologists' Society can provide you with literature, training aides, educational materials, and many other types of assistance as needed. Magazines, newspapers, radio, television and documentary videos (available at your local video store) are also sources of information. For other specific suggestions, refer to the Resources section near the end of this manual.

Your greatest asset is your own ingenuity. You are not expected to know everything. Help is available from Y.E.S. staff, advisors, and other teachers when you need it.

Working With Youth

What do they want to learn? What do you want to teach? Many people think of entomology as making an insect collection. It is in fact much broader than this! There are numerous opportunities for youth to learn about entomological science without making a collection. One of the primary purposes of this manual is to open your eyes to these hundreds of alternative possibilities.

Another thing to keep in mind is that not all the activities or learning experiences on insects have to produce tangible results. Get the children involved in activities that are actually learning disguised as fun. For example, play a game, make an insect craft, or spend time watching insects in their natural environment.

When working with young people you are encouraged to:
· Make it fun and make it participatory!
· Be flexible; allow plenty of time for experimentation.
· Help youth build creativity, confidence and positive values; encourage children to solve problems on their own.
· Appreciate the natural expression of each child. Give each youth opportunities to make decisions and do things their way.
· Provide recognition for project or personal development. Recognize children for doing good work. Remember to always praise in public and correct (criticize) in private.
· Utilize outside resources for extra stimulation.
· **Don't be a teacher who uses activities:**
  - with involuntary "Its"
  - that doesn't give members a chance to "pass"
  - that are put-downs or put people on the spot
  - that encourage the group to laugh <u>at</u> someone rather than <u>with</u> someone
  - that are "fun" at someone's expense
  - that are exclusive (musical chairs), or give an advantage to physical stature, age, or gender
  - that use competition that may pull the group apart

Understanding the Developmental Needs of Children

One of the first things you will want to consider when planning insect instruction is the age, experience level, and size of your group. Keep in mind that the attention span, comprehension level, hand-eye coordination, and interests are going to vary greatly between children of different age groups. To get you started, I have made general suggestions of appropriate activities and projects for younger youth (preschool through grade 5). Information for older youth can be found in Project B.U.G.S. - Level II. Details on specific lesson and project ideas can be found in the lessons and activities section of this manual.

Working with 3 and 4 year olds. Yes, even toddlers and preschoolers can be exposed to the amazing world of insects! You will have the best luck teaching them about insects through play, finger plays, singing songs, movement activities, puppets, stories, poems, and action rhymes. Watch the group closely to monitor their attention span; have lots of backup ideas if something goes more quickly than planned, or is a dud. Don't be afraid to play act and pretend. If you talk about an insect, be that insect! Of course you will need to avoid big words, or at least explain those for which you can't come up with simpler alternatives. Oh, and don't forget to include plenty of time for them to talk and share.
Some important educational goals for 3 and 4 year olds include:
· Form positive attitudes about insects.
· Recognize different types of insect movement.
· Learn basic facts about insects.
Some activities you may wish to consider for 3 and 4 year olds include:
· Make simple insect models using household materials.
· Make and use insect puppets.
· Color pictures of insects and make an insect art gallery.
· Try some finger plays, songs, rhymes, or chants.
· Read (and talk about) a short insect story.
· Movement games and activities (pretending to be insects, caterpillar race, busy bee, etc.).
· Take a walk to look and listen for insects.

Working with 5 to 8 year olds. When working with children in the 5 to 8 year old age group you will find that they have a natural curiosity about everything. They are also willing to try almost anything. For this reason they are the ideal stage for learning about the insect world! You should have a wide variety of action experiences (hands-on) planned for your 5 to 8 year old children. Be sure to make these experiences cooperative, not competitive. Don't expect to hold their attention for longer than 10 minutes at a time while giving instructions or other information. Plan for activities that they can do together. Watch for children who are loners and find ways for them to be part of the group. It is also advised that there be one adult or teen helper for every 6 children. Also keep in mind that they have not refined their fine motor skills, and they will need lots of practice using pencils, crayons, scissors, and other small tools (such as forceps and insect pins). Most of them can read some words, but remember that reading may still be a mystery to some of them. Other children can read many things and will consume whole books.
Some important educational goals for 5 to 8 year olds include:
· Use simple measuring devices.
· Practice skills for information gathering and problem solving.
·.Construct simple charts and graphs (of childrens' favorite insects, for example).
· Show how science concepts can be interpreted through creative expressions, such as language arts, music, and fine arts.
· Develop an awareness of and sensitivity to the world of insects.
· Describe the functions of selected insect body parts.

- Compare and classify familiar insects on the basis of observable physical characteristics.
- Describe the life cycle of familiar insects (grasshopper, dragonfly, and butterfly).
- Explain how fossils provide evidence about insects from long ago.
- Describe the basic requirements for insects (and all living things) to maintain their existence.
- Compare and contrast food, energy, and habitat needs of familiar insects.
- Explain common patterns of interdependence and interrelationships of insects and other living things.
- Identify familiar insects as part of a food chain (or web) and describe their feeding relationships within the web.
- Describe the positive and negative effects of humans on the habitats of insects.
- Discuss familiar insect products (honey and silk) and services (pollination/seed production).

Some activities you may wish to consider for 5 to 8 year olds include:
- Make insect models using household and recycled materials.
- Make and use insect puppets.
- Make a bulletin board of insect pictures highlighting insect colors, shapes, life cycles, behavior, habitats or other themes.
- Make and decorate homemade bug cages out of old pop bottles, milk jugs, tuna cans and rolled screening, etc.
- Make simple collecting equipment like a net and bug "barn".
- Try some arts and crafts: decoupage using insect pictures; block or sponge printing; rubber stamp pictures; insect life cycle mobile; bug masks; insect stencils.
- Draw and/or color pictures of insects and make an insect art gallery.
- Make jigsaw puzzles (cut up insect picture to put back together).
- Try the insect "alphabet" - name an insect for each letter of the alphabet (a great group activity).
- Try some songs, rhymes, or tongue twisters.
- Try acting out some stories, skits or plays about insects.
- Read (and talk about) an insect or spider story.
- Play board games, card games or insect bingo.
- Movement games and activities (caterpillar race, busy bee, etc.).
- Keep an insect as a "pet" for a couple of weeks.
- Start a simple butterfly garden with a few butterfly plants.
- Take a walk to look and listen for insects.

Working with pre-adolescents. Children in this age group desire a sense of independence, yet they want and need guidance from adults. To provide balance between these two opposing needs, a teacher can put more emphasis on children getting assistance from older youth, other teachers, parents, and peers. Another characteristic of this age group is desire for group activity, so you might have them work in small groups. With the younger members of this group (9 to 12 years old) you may find it best to separate boys and girls for project work since this age group tends to be with members of their own sex.

Teachers with pre-adolescents should try to outline "things to do" in detail. Make recordkeeping simple and ask for short narrative reports that will prompt children to review what they have learned.

Some important educational goals for pre-adolescents include:
- Design and conduct simple investigations on insects.
- Use measuring devices to provide consistency in insect investigations.

- Use sources of information to help solve problems or answer questions about insects.
- Write and follow procedures in the form of step-by-step instructions, flow diagrams, identification keys, and sketches.
- Show how insect science and technology apply in real-world contexts.
- Recognize the contributions made by insect scientists of diverse backgrounds.
- Compare and classify insects and other arthropods into major groups based on their structure.
- Describe how the characteristics of insects are passed on from generation to generation.
- Describe how heredity and environment may influence/determine the characteristics of an insect.
- Describe how biologists might trace possible evolutionary relationships among present and past insect forms.
- Describe common patterns of relationships among populations of insects and other animals.
- Predict the effects of changes in one population in a food web on populations of other animals and plants.
- Describe ways in which humans alter the environment, thereby effecting insect populations.
- Explain how humans use and benefit from insect products and services.

Some activities you may wish to consider for pre-adolescents include:
- Make a poster, bulletin board or display of insect pictures (or insect artifacts) highlighting insect colors, shapes, life cycles, behavior, habitats or other themes.
- Put together a list of trivia questions on insects.
- Make and use a quiz board on insects.
- Build bug cages, spreading boards, collection boxes, nets, or other homemade entomology equipment.
- Learn how to make and arrange collections (adult insects, immatures, or non-insects; gall-making insects; aquatic insects; insect stamps; insect nests or homes (actual or photographs).
- Make some insect wing laminations (wings sandwiched between clear contact paper).
- Embed insects or other arthropods in plastic.
- Visit a large entomological collection or insect museum.
- Observe a flower plant, beehive, or ant hill. Take notes or photographs of the activity observed.
- Set up a temporary insect zoo of native insects.
- Rear an insect and observe and record their life cycle.
- Design and plant a butterfly garden (or study the plants that attract butterflies in your area).
- Investigate the origin of insect scientific names.
- Explore the use of insects as objects of art, music, literature, religion, and folklore.
- Find out where different insects spend the winter.
- Find out what states have official state insects.
- Prepare an article on insect collecting, insect rearing, insect behavior or any other interesting facet of entomology for publication in INSECT WORLD published by the Young Entomologists' Society (see the appendix).
- Prepare a short story or a poem for publication in INSECT WORLD.
- Create crossword puzzles, wordfinds or other puzzles using entomological terms and submit them for publication in INSECT WORLD (see appendix).

TEACHING STRATEGIES AND METHODS

Most learners (both youth and adults) will respond better if at least some of the learning is "by doing" and if a variety of methods are used. As a general rule, **people learn:**

10% of what they read ... 20% of what they hear ...
30% of what they see ... 50% of what they see and hear ...
60% of what they discuss with others ...
80% of what they experience personally ...
and 90% of what they teach someone else!

In order to teach for retention of information, consider these seven guiding principles:

· Determine the knowledge that each child possesses about insects so you can gear your teaching to their needs.
· Relate to the children's level (talk about butterflies instead of Lepidoptera, and bugs instead of insects).
· Use positive transfer (relate a new subject to something they have already done or know and present it in an organized manner).
· Present quality, not quantity of information (for most children, adequate coverage of a few topics is more satisfying than superficial coverage of many topics; stress concepts, not facts).
· Practice and more practice (give children opportunities to use their new knowledge; success is a strong motivational tool).
· Behaviors and learning that are reinforced (rewarded) are more likely to be learned (and must follow as immediately as possible the desired behavior).
· Give students a chance to be "teacher" through displays, discussions, and demonstrations.

The following are some helpful teaching techniques to use in your teaching and activities:

Hands-on Activities. Lessons should include at least one or two hands-on activities, where students can manipulate the objects they are studying (insect artifacts, etc.) and handle and use scientific instruments (rulers, balances, microscopes, collecting equipment, etc.). However, in the larger context "hands-on" is learning by doing, and can include arts and crafts, theme snacks, science experiments, creating insect zoos, insect collecting, making equipment, and the like. "Real life" experiences, like planting a butterfly garden or caring for live insects, and problem-solving experiences are also extremely valuable teaching tools for working with youth. Use these whenever you can.

While the term "hands-on" is a frequently used one, try to select activities that help children explore the world with all five of their senses - tasting, hearing, smelling, seeing, and touching. Help them use their eyes, ears, noses, and taste buds, and not just their fingers, to better understand the insect world.

Seeing Insects. Most people study the insect world using this dominant sense. Still, we seldom take time to carefully study the sizes, shapes, and colors of insects. If you are lucky enough to have access to some insect collections, have the children spend time observing the shapes and colors of insects. Or, observe insects in their natural habitat or in captivity. Can they identify any patterns? (For example, can the various body shapes be categorized based on similarities and differences?) Make a list of the colors seen. What are the purposes for some of these colors? Which colors are for warning other animals? (black/yellow and black/orange) Which colors and shapes are used for camouflage? (Play the "Aphid Alley", "Great Moth Hunt", or "Walkingstick Jungle" games, page 89.).

appropriate)   Take the time to watch insects move. How do they walk,
run, or fly? Also, watch insects while they gather their food. What do
they eat and how do they eat it?

Use binoculars or spotting scopes to watch large, active insects like
butterflies and dragonflies. Use magnifiers (hand lens or microscope, if
appropriate) and offer the children opportunities for close inspection of
tiny insects (like aphids, fleas, and ants) and insect artifacts. Cameras
and video camcorders can be used to record your observations on film or
videotape (a great way to share your observations with others).

Hearing Insects. Many insects make audible sounds. Bees, flies,
mosquitoes, grasshoppers, crickets, cicadas, and some beetles can all be
heard. What are these sounds used for? (warning, attracting mates) You
may want to make some sound recordings of insects. You will need a
portable tape recorder, microphone and patch cord, and a long stick (or an
old umbrella). The real trick is getting the microphone close enough to
the insect to record the sound, but at the same time not disturbing it.
If you attach the microphone to the end of a long pole you can usually
accomplish this task in a satisfactory manner. An alternative method is
to use an old umbrella as a parabolic reflector to amplify the sound made
by the insect. Attach the microphone to the handle (facing the inside of
the umbrella) about 6 inches (15cm) from the apex. Depending on the exact
shape of your umbrella it may be necessary to adjust the position of the
microphone up or down the handle; monitor the incoming sound to find the
best position. Furthermore, if you spray the inside of the umbrella with
a thin layer of metallic silver paint the sound gathering capability of
your homemade parabolic reflector should be significantly increased. To
use the parabolic reflector and microphone, hold the umbrella by its tip
and point the open "dish" towards the singing insect.

If you are unable or unwilling to make your own recordings, examples
of some insect songs are available on prerecorded cassette tapes. "A
Guide to Night Sounds" by Lang Elliott (NatureSound Studio, Ithaca, NY,
1992.) features the songs of the snowy tree cricket, mole cricket, ground
cricket, katydid, cone-head grasshopper, and pine sawyer.

Also, many insect sounds can be imitated by children, either vocally
or with simple instruments (like a comb and pencil to produce a katydid
call). Electronic devices are also available that reproduce the call of a
cricket or the shrill song of a cicada.

Feeling Insects. Children love to touch whatever they're looking at,
and insects are no exception. Both living and dead insects can be used to
find out how insects feel. The exoskeletons of insects have many
textures: smooth, rough, waxy, hairy, and spiny, just to name a few. Are
butterfly wings really "buttery" and slippery? What does it feel like to
have an insect walk across your hand? You might also want to explore the
texture of the paper made by wasps, the honeycomb made by bees, or the
tunnels made by woodboring insects. To really get children to use their
sense of touch without interference from the eyes, place rubber bugs or
real insect artifacts (galls, wasp paper, fossils, tunneled wood, etc.) in
a "What is it Box". This can be made from a cardboard carton with a
flapdoor in the back and a sleeved hole in the front.

Smelling Insects. Yes, many insects have distinctive odors! Like
tiny, six-legged "skunks" many insects use special odorous chemicals to
repel would-be enemies. Insects like giant (Blaberus) cockroaches, stink
bugs, ground beetles, and certain tiger beetles all have distinctive
odors. Other insects, like butterflies and moths, use special chemical
odors known as pheromones to communicate with each other. These chemicals
are released in such small amounts that they cannot be detected by
humans. Mosquitoes and other biting flies use chemical odors to find

warm-blooded animals. They are able to locate the "clouds" of carbon dioxide produced by larger animals and zero in on the target for a blood meal.

Tasting Insects. Many people have never willingly tasted an insect, although most of us love to eat their crustacean relatives (shrimp, crayfish, crabs, and lobsters). However, in many countries and cultures insects are considered a delicacy. And they're good for you too, about 90-95% protein! I'm not suggesting that you eat every insect that you see, however many different species are quite tasty. Most insects should be cooked before being eaten and recipes can be found in books such as "Butterflies in My Stomach" by Ronald Taylor (Woodbridge Press, Santa Barbara, CA. 1975.) or "Entertaining with Insects" by Ronald Taylor (Woodbridge Press, Santa Barbara, CA. 1976.) Every one has heard of chocolate covered ants, but how about "Cricket Lickets" or "Hot Licks"? (These are lollipops that have a cricket or tequila worm embedded in the candy.) There is even a restaurant in Washington, DC that specializes in insect cuisine! An interesting story on this theme is "Beetles Lightly Toasted" by Phyliss Naylor (Atheneum, New York. 1987.) A "Food Insect Newsletter" is also available from the Department of Entomology, Russell Labs, University of Wisconsin, Madison, WI 53706. And don't forget about that tasty treat made by bees - honey!

If the thought of eating real insects doesn't appeal to you, why not substitute insect theme snacks. Here are some examples. Ants on a Log: Cut celery stalks into four to six inch pieces. Fill the concave side with peanut butter; place several raisins on the peanut butter. Butterfly Cookies: Use butterfly-shaped cookie cutters to cut the dough before baking these cookies. Decorate to taste. Insects in Amber: Following package directions, mix two large boxes of orange or lemon gelatin. After the gelatin is completely dissolved in the hot water, pour gelatin into small cups or ice cube trays. Add a few raisins to represent insects in each piece of "amber". Let the gelatin cool and set. To remove the gelatin from the mold, run hot water over the outside of the container(s) for 10 to 15 seconds. Ladybugs: Spread strawberry jam on a hamburger bun and decorate with raisins (the spots, of course). Butterfly Jigglers: You can use butterfly and bug-shaped cookie cutters to make Jell-O Jigglers (TM). In addition to the cookie cutters you will need 4 small boxes (or 2 large boxes) of gelatin, a 13 x 9" pan, and boiling water. Stir boiling water into gelatin according to package directions. Pour mixture slowly into 13 x 9" pan. (For easiest removal, lightly coat pan with a cooking spray before pouring in the gelatin mixture.) Chill at least 3 hours. Jigglers will be firm after one hour, but may difficult to remove from the pan. To cut Jigglers, dip the bottom of the pan in warm water for 15 seconds to loosen gelatin. Cut shapes with cookie cutters all the way through the gelatin. Lift from the pan with index finger or metal spatula. Marshmallow Creepy Crawlies: Use pretzel sticks to assemble three marshmallows into a "bug". The pretzel sticks are also used as the legs and antennae.

Participatory Activities. These types of activities (games, drama, songs, and excursions) are favorites with younger youth (but work well with older youth, too.). Interactive games and movement games can play an important role in the smooth operation of your classes. Movement games can help younger youth expend some of their abundant energy and settle down for other activities. Drama (skits, storytelling, poems, and role playing) and songs provide an outlet for creative expression in children while teaching about insects at the same time (see references, pages 35, 38, and 39). Participatory activities suitable for small groups include card games, board games, science experiments, and books/stories. Contests are also a type of "game" that you can use with older youth; <u>never</u> use competition with younger youth.

Dramatic Play Centers and Insect Learning Centers. Younger children learn a great deal through dramatic play. As they play and act out different scenarios, they have opportunities to use materials in new ways, encountering problem-solving challenges that help build critical-thinking skills. During the course of dramatic play with other children a child has the opportunity to practice cooperation, communication, coordination (exercising small and large muscles), and science skills (counting and sorting). Dramatic play can be encouraged by setting up an "Insect Study Laboratory", featuring insect artifacts and replicas, posters, magnifiers and other equipment (like plastic forceps, bug bottles, critter extractors, and nets), manipulatives and toys, puppets, puzzles, books, notebooks and pencils (or crayons and markers), coloring sheets, lab coats and hats (with Young Entomologists' patch).

A more formal learning center on insects for older children should include a variety of equipment and materials, such as insect artifacts, aquaria for indoor microhabitats (including potting soil, sand, vegetation and sticks) and live insects, worksheets and coloring sheets, games, posters, rubber stamps and stickers, plenty of books, audio and video tapes, nets, bug bottles, magnifiers, and trays for sorting. Encourage the children to work individually or in small groups to explore the items in the Insect Learning Center. Provide guidance by suggesting they count or sort items, observe artifacts closely, or get creative with rubber stamps, stickers, or drawings. Or, organize materials into activity kits; for example, bring together a book, rubber replica, and artifact for each of several common insects, or the materials needed for a simple experiment or other activity. To make the area official, don't forget to make an attractive sign for your "Insect Learning Center". Try to have a mixture of both fiction and non-fiction books so that the children will begin to recognize that some books should be read when wanting to learn facts (nonfiction), while others should be read for pleasure (fiction). Encourage the children to browse through the books and select titles for silent reading times.

Selecting developmentally appropriate educational materials will promote social, emotional, intellectual, and physical development while considering the children's interests, capabilities, needs and backgrounds. When choosing materials for dramatic play and learning centers, keep the following criteria in mind: (1) Is the item durable and safe, (2) Is the item too challenging or too easy (designed to keep children interested and adaptable to varying developmental needs), (3) Is the item flexible in use (preferably multi-sensory and open-ended to encourage creative thinking and exploration), (4) Are materials concrete instead of abstract (interactive and collaborative), and (5) Are materials anti-bias (represent multicultural diversity - people of different races, sexes, abilities, and cultural backgrounds).

Field Studies and Observations. Field observations of live insects can be extremely interesting. Children may gain valuable insight into how insects interact with one another and with other insects, animals and plants (ecology). Many interesting facts about insect life cycles, behavior, and ecology will be discovered by observing insects in their natural habitat. Field observations can be made on insect development and life cycles, insect behavior, and on insect populations and communities. (When making field observations, scientists always record their observations in a notebook or journal. To reinforce the importance of this skill, have the children keep a simple insect journal. Important information that should be recorded includes date, location, conditions, observations, and names of observers. Some observations are better recorded as photographs or video tape. Sound recordings also may be used to gather information on those insects which "sing" or make other sounds.)

Field Trips. A field trip is an excellent class activity and also a way to provide members with "hands-on" experience and expand their knowledge and interest in entomology. (A field trip where students participate in an activity or other hands-on experience is far more valuable than one where they simply go to see a demonstration or talk!) A trip requires some prior planning, but it can be well worth the effort. Early planning will allow time for making any necessary arrangements. (If you're going on an insect "safari" to observe or collect insects it's always to good idea to explore the area ahead of time so that you can check for special features or potential problems.) On the day prior to the field trip, discuss with the children what they can expect to see or do and any special equipment or clothing they will need to bring with them. If appropriate, discuss the rules on behavior while on a field trip: (1) stay within sight of the group at all times (use the buddy system), (2) no playing in any water, (3) no tree, wall, or fence climbing, (4) no poking or horseplay with nets, (5) no "shoving" insects and spiders into people's faces, and (6) return all rocks, logs and other "bug" habitat to their original condition after looking for insects. Remind the children that some insects sting and bite, so they should be careful when trying to coax an insect into a jar or get it out of a net. Additional suggestions and tips for outdoor collecting trips can be found on page 20.

For other types of field trips it is strongly recommended that you determine whether or not the host facility and staff can provide an orderly, efficient, and structured experience for the children that features good scientific content and appropriate methods of instruction. Your time away from the classroom is valuable and expensive, so you want to be certain the children will be exposed to a quality experience.

The following are some examples of the types of field trips you could take:

- Take a simple walk in your schoolyard or neighborhood to see what types of insects live there. To sharpen observation skills and reinforce math skills (counting, sorting, pattern recognition, comparing, and analyzing), play "I Spy" while on your walk. Challenge the children to find insects with no wings/2 wings/4 wings, find insects smaller/bigger than a ladybug, insects that are green/blue/red/yellow, insects that are round/elongate, leaves eaten by insects, insect nests and webs, or different groups of insects (beetles/flies/butterflies/true bugs).
- Take a trip to a few different types of habitats (woods, gardens, orchards, fields, ponds, streams, or parks) or to the same habitat under different circumstances, such as different seasons or day vs. night. (Later, compare how the insects of each habitat were different and similar.)
- Take a cocoon (or mantis egg mass) collecting trip in the winter and watch the cocoons (eggs) hatch the following spring.
- Take a trip to a natural history museum, science museum, insect zoo, butterfly house, or butterfly garden. If possible, arrange to have the group take a "behind the scenes" look so they can see how the facility manages its collection and/or live insects. Insect zoos and butterfly houses are a wonderful way to explore the insects of other countries, and to see insects from far away places. You can help children understand the roles that insects play in the lives of people in other countries. A complete list of suitable facilities can be found in the "Insect Study Sourcebook" by Gary A. Dunn (see bibliography).

· Visit a university entomology department, government agriculture/ forestry facility, pesticide research center, or pest control company for a first hand look at current entomological concerns and research. Explore possible career opportunities in entomology.
· Tour a beekeeping farm and see how honey is made.

Followup activities are an important part of a field trip experience. Allow time for the children to exchange observations, experiences and ideas. Be sure to follow up on any unanswered questions with library research. You might want to schedule group or individual reports (oral, written, or displays). Or, supply each child with a list of insect-related "observations" to make while they are on the field trip. For example, have them record the results of their observations to questions such as "how many bee hives where there at the beekeeping farm", or "at the insect zoo, what is the country of origin for the hissing cockroach".

Guest Speakers. If a field trip is out of the question, you might want to consider arranging for a guest entomologist to visit with the children. A visiting scientist can help children understand the positive and vital role of entomological science, gain an understanding of the work scientists do, see scientists as real people, and lay a foundation for considering careers in science. Consult "The Insect Study Sourcebook" (see bibliography) to see if there is an insect outreach program in your area. You may also be able to locate a speaker by contacting local entomologists (professional and amateur), beekeepers, pest control operators, county extension staff, high school teachers, college faculty, and other interested adults in your community (or nearby). One word of caution, however. Make sure your speaker is familiar with the needs of children and able to offer information on their level!

Audio-Visuals. Audio-visuals (movies, slides, computer games, etc.) can bring great excitement to the classroom by "introducing" children to other presenters and experiences that may not be available locally.

Demonstrations and "Show and Tell". These are particularly useful teaching techniques for the entomology area. A demonstration is simply showing and telling other children how to do something. Encourage the children to give at least one demonstration during the insect unit to fellow students or other classes. These can be simple, informal demonstrations which will get the children more actively involved in their own learning. For a little variety, try mixing individual presentations and team presentations (3-4 children). Topics for demonstrations and speeches can include insect habitats, collecting techniques, preserving and mounting, insect identification, insect rearing, beekeeping, and careers in entomology. Other topics will no doubt come up in the course of conducting lessons or activities. The list of possibilities is nearly endless! Of course you can also invite parents and other resource people to demonstrate or talk about specific topics when appropriate.

Most of us are familiar with the concept of "show and tell", which is really just a simple type of demonstration and sharing. Of course this method can be used with even young children, although it is probably better to call it "sharing time" or "children's teaching time" to avoid the pitfalls of favorite toys and pets. Show the children that they can be the "teacher", with something to offer that help others learn about insects. Encourage them to share insect artifacts they have found, live critters (to release when done), pictures and photographs, a favorite bug book, or collecting equipment.

Computer Simulations and Demonstrations. There are many computer software programs that feature insects and insect information. If you have access to computer hardware it would be possible to allow the children to try out some of this educational software.

Software you might want to try for younger children includes "SimAnt" by Maxis (2 Theatre Square, Suite 230, Orinda, CA 94563-3041, or 800-33-MAXIS), "Bug Adventure" by Knowledge Adventure (4502 Dyer Street, La Crescenta CA 91214, or 818-542-4200), or "Creepy Crawlies" by Sony Electronic Publishing (c/o Fas-Track Computer Products, 7030C Huntley Road, Columbus, OH 43229-1053, or 800-927-3936). Other educational software on insects includes "HyperBug" by Entomation (2742 Beacon Hill, Ann Arbor, MI 48104, phone 313-971-6033), "Discovering Insects" and "Food Webs of Insects and their Kin" by Drenkow Media (10306 E. Live Oak Ave., Arcadia, CA 91007), and "Organizing Animals" by Wieser Educational, Inc. (30085 Comercio, Rancho Santa Margarita, CA 92688). Contact local computer stores for assistance in locating other appropriate software.

Experiments. Many interesting facts can be discovered about insect life cycles, behavior, and ecology by experimenting with insects under carefully regulated artificial conditions. Through conducting entomology experiments, children can learn and practice the scientific method. The purpose of the scientific method is to distinguish facts (things that can be proven) from beliefs (things which are only ideas or opinions, and may or may not be true). (After conducting an experiment, children should prepare a report or display to share their results with others.)

Exhibits and Displays. Exhibits and displays give children a chance to show what they've done. Models, collections, photographs, slides, homemade movies, samples of insect artifacts, arts and crafts, and poems and stories, can be used as the basis for an exhibit. Exhibits can also help share important information or ideas with other classes, parents, or the public. Wouldn't that empty showcase down the hall look great filled with insect artifacts and project materials! Bulletin boards in the classroom and hallway should also be used to present information on insects (posters, pictures, etc.) or display student projects (drawings, photographs, poems, etc.).

Lectures and Discussions. The use of lectures, talks, and discussions may have limited success with young people, depending on their age, attention span, and comprehension level. When talking to younger youth (5 to 8 year olds), keep it short and simple. Older youth will be able to handle longer, more complex presentations. Discussions are a way to encourage thought on a subject and can help bring new understanding to complex topics.

Other Tips for Effective Teaching

Use the Discovery Method. Let youth make their own observations and draw their own conclusions. Stimulate their thinking by asking questions. Sometimes your best answer to one of their questions is "I don't know. What do you think? Let's look that up."

Take Advantage of "Teachable Moments". If a relatively rare event occurs (for example, you catch an insect in the act of molting), don't view it as an interruption; instead, use it as an opportunity for at least a brief mention, discussion, or study.

Build a Teaching Team. Co-teach with others whenever possible. Other people have different interests, knowledge, enthusiasms, strengths and teaching styles which will compliment yours and which will appeal to certain youth.

Charts and Graphs. Use plenty of charts and graphs because these help bring the world into sharper focus for children. Graphs help children understand concepts like similarities and differences, comparisons, numbers, estimations, and graph analysis. You can use graphs to present information on all kinds of insect topics: insects by habitat, insects by body parts (wings, legs, mouthparts), insect development (types of metamorphosis), favorite insects, insects by color, insects by size, mosquito bites per person (set time limit), butterflies in the garden on a daily basis, or favorite insect books.

Challenge Your Youth and Let Them Take the Lead. Don't let them stop after learning the basics. Let them thoroughly explore topics of great interest to them.

Involve Parents and Other Adults. Don't forget to invite the involvement of parents and other adults (relatives and friends). Some of them may be employed in entomology-related careers (beekeeping, pest control, research, etc.); others may have access to insect artifacts or equipment that you can borrow. All parents can assist in helping you "scrounge" for insect study equipment and supplies (like spoons, eyedroppers, kitchen strainers, empty peanut butter jars, tuna/catfood cans, screening, fossils, insect artifacts, magazine/calendar pictures, film canisters, straws, arts and crafts materials, paper towel tubes, fact books and story books on insects, etc.). All you need to do is ask - parents and other adults are often all too glad to help in such an easy, meaningful way.

Protect Your Teaching Materials. Most teachers are familiar with and have access to a laminating machine. Photographs, pictures, and other 2-dimensional artifacts need to be protected so that they will last for many years. If you do not have access to a laminating machine, most copy stores can do the job for you at a reasonable cost. Or, use clear contact paper and laminate it yourself!

Awards and Incentives. Exhibiting completed projects at school, a local community center, library, science fair, shopping mall, or other public place provides recognition to the child, and helps increase public awareness about the importance of insects.

Don't underestimate the importance of giving lots of verbal praise for all children's accomplishments. For those special occasions where a prize or incentive is called for, you can design a certificate, make "Bug Nut Trophies" (see page 116), or purchase a special gift. The Young Entomologists' Society has a variety of inexpensive items (patches, buttons, pencils, bookmarks, etc.) that can be used as rewards.

INNOVATIVE IDEAS FOR TEACHING ABOUT INSECTS

RUBBER "BUGS" IN THE CLASSROOM

Rubber "bugs" (insects, spiders, and other arthropods) are readily available from toy or novelty stores, or the Young Entomologists' Society, and they can be used educationally in many creative ways. Obviously, as inanimate objects rubber "bugs" are ideal for use as substitute experimental animals: they are virtually indestructible, are always cooperative, never need food or water, and don't bite, sting or smell!

Here are a few examples of ways that you can use rubber "bugs" in your teaching. You can probably think of other ways to use these versatile educational tools.

Rubber "Bugs" in Science Lessons

Insect Anatomy. You can use rubber bugs to illustrate many of the important insect body structures like head, thorax, abdomen, antennae, compound eyes, mouthparts, wings, legs, etc. Later on you can ask students to "name the parts". You may want to point out variations (adaptations) of some body parts and how these help insects (legs for running vs. legs for jumping, or wings for flying vs. wings for protection). ✳How are spiders and other arthropods different from insects? ✳

Sorting, Classifying, and Identifying. Observe how similarities and differences in overall shape and body appendages (mouthparts, legs, and wings) allow us to sort and classify insects into groups of similar types. Learn how us make and use dichotomous identification keys. Many rubber "bugs" are anatomically correct, so can you identify your rubber specimens (are they a grasshopper, beetle, fly, spider or other arthropod). For an added challenge, project the outlines of the rubber "bugs" using an overhead projector or shadow box and see if your group can identify them by shape alone.

Insect Behavior. The color and shape of many insects makes it easy to conceal themselves from their enemies or prey (camouflage). What evidence of this behavior do you see in your rubber "bugs". Have an indoor or outdoor "bug" hunt. Place the rubber "bugs" in a simulated area of habitat (classroom or school yard) and see which insects are most easily found.

Insect Ecology. Set up four four representative "habitats" (green carpeting = grassland, sand = desert, potted plants = forest, and blue paper/foil = water). See if the students can assign the rubber "bugs" to the proper habitat using clues like body part adaptations and/or prior knowledge. Or, categorize the insects by food preferences (plant feeders, predators, or scavengers). Then you can follow this up by constructing a representative food web (food chain/food pyramid) using rubber arthropods and other animals.

Making Fossil Replicas. You can easily demonstrate how animal remains become fossils by pressing a rubber "bug" into wet plaster of Paris (held in place within a shallow pan), Plasticine, or modeling clay. This results in a reverse (negative) impression of the fossilized animal. Have each child make several impressions with different insects, and then ask the group members if they can figure out which insect made each impression (to show how scientists can identify ancient animals by the impressions they left behind). If you coat this reverse impression with salad oil or petroleum jelly, you can then cast a positive impression that looks just like the original critter that was fossilized, its' body replaced by minerals (the plaster).

Rubber "Bugs" in Math Lessons

Counting, Estimating and Other Math Skills. Practice counting or estimating with assortments of small rubber "bugs". Obtain a collection of small plastic "eggs" and fill them with assorted numbers of small rubber bugs. Have the children select several eggs and count the number of "bugs" found in each egg. Graph the results, or add the counts to get a total for each child. Average the totals for all the children, or determine the highest and lowest counts (range).

Measuring. Practice measuring the length of the rubber "bugs" (or parts of them: antennae, legs, wings, etc.). Discuss why standards of measurement are important (all must measure the length of the body plus the antennae, or just the body to have comparable measurements). Measure in English vs. metric. If you have "bugs" of different sizes, calculate the largest, smallest, and average. You may want to graph the results for better visualization.

Weighing. Practice weighing the rubber "bugs" with scales. Weigh in English vs. metric. If you have "bugs" of different weights, calculate the heaviest, lightest, and average. You may want to graph the results for better visualization.

Rubber "Bugs" in Arts and Crafts Lessons

Models for Drawing. Rubber "bugs" can be used as models for making life-like drawings of insects or other arthropods. If the images and outlines of rubber "bugs" are projected with an overhead or opaque projector, their enlarged outlines can be traced.

Dioramas. Rubber "bugs" make great props for educational dioramas and displays. Rubber "bugs" can be used in realistic habitat dioramas made from dried plant parts, sand/soil, or stones. Or, make decorative arrangements using dried flowers, plant parts, driftwood, or stones, and then add some rubber "bugs".

Mobiles. Assemble a collection of rubber "bugs" into a mobile. What a great way to learn about balance and the fulcrum!

Rubber "Bugs" in Language Arts and Communications

Subjects for Writing. Rubber "bugs" can be used as subjects for descriptive writing. Have the children prepare a written description of one or more of the rubber "bugs". Have the children read their description and see if the group can figure out which one is being described. Or, write a story about one of the rubber "bugs" that magically comes to life one day. Give each child a small plastic jar filled with a different assortment of small rubber critters (insects, spiders, and other animals) and a variety of other trinkets (such as play money, string, figurines, toy cars, boats or planes, buttons, beads, etc.). Have each child make up a story (written or verbal) using the objects from their jar.

Storytelling. Rubber "bugs" can be used as an aid to storytelling and as library "book companions" (book lists on pages 29 through 39).

Rubber "Bugs" in Child Development and Life Skills

Observation Skills. Place a variety of rubber "bugs" on the table and let the children look at them briefly. Then cover them up and ask them to make a list of all the rubber "bugs" they can remember seeing.

Matching Exercises. Pair identical or similar bugs and ask children to identify which sets are alike and which sets are not alike.

Familiarization with Insects. Many insect phobias can be partially or wholly eliminated through the use of rubber "bugs". Discuss why some people are afraid of insects and spiders.

Healthy Attitudes About Insects. Rubber "bugs" can be used to help children acquire a healthy, realistic attitude towards insects and other arthropods.

Manual Dexterity and Motor Skills. Young children can use the rubber "bugs" as manipulatives to improve manual dexterity and motor skills. Hide an assortment of rubber "bugs" in oatmeal, rice, unpopped popcorn kernals, sawdust, or clean sand or gravel. Give the children an opportunity to "dig" for the hidden critters. Or, give children a selection of small rubber bugs, a pair of plastic tweezers, and an empty peanut butter jar. Let them pretend to be an entomologist and pick up the insects with the tweezers and drop them into the jar (or ants in an anthill, or bees in a hive, etc.).

Creative Play. Rubber "bugs" can be a welcome prop for creative play and stretching the imagination. Because of their durability they can be used as water toys (bath tub) or sand box toys. I even know of one person who used a rubber lobster as a practical joke in their hot tub! Make an imaginary "insect zoo" using the rubber "bugs". Have the children be zookeepers and make signs with the names of the insects and important "care" instructions.

Miscellaneous Rubber "Bugs" Activities

Games. Rubber "bugs", especially the smaller ones, can be used as game pieces in a wide variety of board games. How many games can you and the children create that incorporate rubber "bugs" and learning about insects?

OBSERVING AND COLLECTING INSECTS

Depending on the amount of time available and the size of your group(s), you may or may not want to include observing or collecting insects in your insect study unit. Observing and/or collecting insects will often enable children to learn a good deal more about the species of insects that live in their area. By locating live insects in their natural habitats they will learn firsthand about life stages, behavior, and habitat affinities. When they observe (and/or collect) insects they will see for themselves the abundance and diversity of insect species that live all around them. Who knows, their observations could also provide insights into some of the many unanswered questions about insects! However, one word of caution about collections. It is also possible to collect several hundred different types of insects at a porch light (enough to make a very impressive collection!), yet the collector has learned very little about insects, except for the fact that some species are attracted to lights!

The first step in observing (and possibly collecting) insects is know something of their food habits and where and how they live. One of the nice things about insects is that with so many species inhabiting our planet, you can look in just about any habitat type and find many interesting insects. Your observations of insects will be most fruitful if you choose a place with special insect habitat, like flowering plants. Insect nests are another "hotspot" where there will be plenty of insect activity. Detailed information on when, where, and how to find insects, as well as suggestions for observation activities and projects, can be found in "A Beginner's Guide to Observing and Collecting Insects" by Gary A. Dunn (Young Entomologists' Society, Lansing, MI. 1994.). Specific suggestions and instructions for observing a variety of insects can be found in the lessons and activities section of this manual under the topics of Insect Behavior (page 87) and Insect Ecology (page 96).

Many types of standard insect collecting equipment can be used to assist with insect observations. For example, bug bottles, nets, forceps, aspirators, and field notebooks are just as important to insect observers as they are to insect collectors. Of course, insects that are collected need not necessarily be killed; live insects in captivity can be used for close study and observation, behavioral and ecological experiments, and for rearing.

TO COLLECT OR NOT TO COLLECT?

The question of whether or not to make an insect collection is as much an ethical issue as it is a scientific issue. In the end, the decision to collect or not collect insects is a personal decision, and both positions have merit.

Those who choose to be an insect collector inevitably hear comments such as "Why do you kill all those wonderful insects?". Comments such as these are usually based on a common misconception, that insect collectors destroy huge numbers of insects and are at least partially responsible for the decline in the populations of butterflies and other familiar insects. The truth is that no dedicated, environmentally ethical collector has ever set out to destroy as many insect as possible.

Why then are there fewer insects today that years ago? The truth is that other human activities have been the culprit. The destruction of insect habitats (including food plants, nectar sources, hibernating sites, etc.) for roads, parking lots, recreation areas, and buildings have killed countless billions of insects. To add insult to injury, these areas of human development rarely include replacement habitats for insects, only highly manicured lawns and ornamental plantings heavily treated with chemical pesticides. Also, most humans are in favor of insect control programs, from the smallest can of bug spray to the mass aerial spray program. Even though the intent may be to kill only a single type of pest insect, thousands of other species suffer the same fate. Street lights, yard lights and porch lights concentrate large numbers of insects in small areas where they are easily consumed by their natural enemies. Even a simple ride in the country on a warm summer evening will kill more insects by smashing them on the car's grill and windshield than an average collector takes in a month of selective collecting!

The number of insects taken by collectors amounts to less than ten thousandths of one percent of the insects killed by humans, yet from this minute percentage comes all the material used for aesthetic purposes (books, illustrations, and artwork); all the specimens used to compile learning and teaching collections for schools, universities, museums, and public displays; all the documentation on regional diversity, frequency, variability of species, as well as representation in environments undergoing or threatened with alteration by man or natural forces; all the material necessary to compile scientific studies and revisionary works of little known insect groups, plus all the specimens used in scientific work in the fields of agriculture, health, and environmental protection.

And so the collection of insect specimens has long been recognized as an appropriate, valid and necessary activity, well founded in scientific procedure. Furthermore, groups like the Young Entomologists' Society recognize that important contributions can be made to entomological science through the collection of insect specimens by young people and educators, as long as such activity is ecologically sound and within the constraints of appropriate guidelines.

Keeping in mind that insects are a renewable natural resource, it is possible to collect insects for display and study without causing serious harm to insect populations by following a few simple guidelines. (1) The field collecting of insects should be selective and should be limited to sampling, not depleting, populations. When collecting where the size of the population is unknown, caution and restraint should be exercised. When trapping is employed, live traps are preferred to killing traps (which should only be used for planned scientific studies). In any event, all traps should be checked on a regular basis in order to prevent the needless destruction of insects. The use of reared or cultured material for obtaining specimens is encouraged. (2) Collection of insect specimens should be done in ways that minimize damage to the environment (habitat, foodplants, etc.). All insect collectors are obligated to comply with all laws and regulations concerning collection on public lands, protection of rare, threatened or endangered species or habitats, and transportation and importation of both live and preserved material. (More information on this subject can be found in "A Beginner's Guide to Observing and Collecting Insects" by Gary A. Dunn (Young Entomologists' Society, Lansing, MI. 1994.) (3) Collectors are responsible for the preservation of specimens with complete data attached, the proper protection of specimens to ensure their longterm preservation, and the deposition of rare, unusual, or valuable specimens in a university or museum collection. Also, all specimens or collections should be offered to an appropriate scientific institution if a collector losses interest or lacks space to properly store the collection. The Young Entomologists' Society can assist in locating an appropriate depository for collections.

To help you and/or your group decide about the appropriateness of making an insect collection, try reading and discussing the book "The Butterfly Hunt" by Yoshi (Picture Book Studio, Saxonville, MA. 1990.), "Butterfly Night of Old Brown Bear" by Nicholas van Pallandt (Farrar, Straus and Giroux, New York. 1990.), or "Fireflies!" by Julie Brinckloe (Aladdin Books, New York. 1985.). Have the children share feelings about insect collecting and keeping insect "pets". See if the group can come to a consensus about insect collecting.

Generally speaking, I would say that making collections is not appropriate or necessary for preschool and early elementary students. They are much better off participating in observational activities. Now I don't mean that they shouldn't be allowed to collect insects. They'll certainly enjoy the challenges and satisfaction of catching "bugs" to observe. However, after the insects are watched and studied for a while (no more than a day or two), they should be released unharmed in the same area where they were collected.

If you and/or your group are hesitant to collect insects or decide against making a collection of insect specimens, there are some alternative projects that you should consider. Many of these alternatives can be used to provide young people with indirect information on insect diversity, insect behavior, insect habitats, and similar topics.

Class collection alternatives include:
(1) Use existing collections (borrowed from another teacher, a student, a parent, or a nature center) rather than make a new collection.
(2) Make one collection for the entire class (to keep as a reference collection) rather than having each student make a personal collection.
(3) Adopt-a-Collection: find an institution, museum, or organization which is in need of a good insect collection and produce one for them (which you can use in the future).
(4) Make a collection of abandoned insect homes, nests, or other structures.
(5) Make a plaster replica of an insect gall or scale insects on a twig. Press and shape a lump of soft modeling clay into a flat slab. Press a gall, twig or insect body (some hard-bodied beetles can

be used) into the clay. Build a low wall of clay around the perimeter of the slab. Mix some quick-set plaster of Paris and pour it into the mold. Let it set in the mold and when dried, peel the clay away. The plaster block can be painted and mounted for display.

(6) Have the children write a descriptive theme about one (or more) of the insects they have found or seen. Have them describe in detail what they look like, where they were found, how they move, what they eat, etc. Have a few children volunteer read their theme out loud and see if the others can guess what insect is being described.

(7) Make a representative collection of insect replicas (rubber and plastic "bugs").

(8) Make a "collection" of insect pictures (photographs, calendar pictures, magazine pictures, drawings, etc.).

PREPARING FOR A "BUG SAFARI" TO OBSERVE/COLLECT INSECTS

Entomologist's Tool Kit. Have the children create a list of items that they think an insect scientist might need to observe, study, and collect insects in the outdoors. Discuss the use for each type of equipment that the children think of, and fill in with any they may have overlooked.

If you are going to observe or collect insects, here are a few things that I suggest you take along to have a successful trip:

· Collecting jars (a killing jar or two and several empties for livestock). (Note: plastic is better than glass for several reasons, including safety.)
· Plastic ziplock bags or paper sacks for collecting food plants, leaf litter, or other insect artifacts and items.
· Net, if you have one (not absolutely necessary).
· Special collecting tools, as needed: aspirator, beating tray/sheet, forceps/tweezers, trowel, and hand axe).
· Special insect traps, as needed: pitfall trap, bait trap, light trap, and Malaise trap.
· Binoculars for watching butterflies, dragonflies and other large, active insects.
· Magnifiers (magnifying glass, hand lens, field microscope).
· Small notebook, paper and pencils.
· Mosquito repellant.
· Bottle of water to drink.
· First aid kit (at least a couple of band-aids).
· Food (a snack for mid afternoon, or a lunch if out for an extended period).
· Backpack or other cloth bag with shoulder strap or belt straps (to carry equipment and leave your hands free to collect insects).
· Proper clothing (a hat, good shoes, old clothes - pants and long sleeved shirt to protect your legs and arms from berry bushes and other plants; jacket or raincoat, depending on the weather).

HOMEMADE INSECT STUDY EQUIPMENT

Bug Jars. The world's best bug jar can be found on your neighborhood grocer's shelf - the plastic peanut butter jar! Plastic peanut butter jars make ideal bug jars. They are durable and unbreakable (a nice safety attribute); the lids remove easily and the opening is nice and big. They even come filled with a free supply of peanut butter!

   After the peanut butter is gone, soak the jar in hot, soapy water to remove any remaining peanut butter and label. Use a hot nail or drill to make 10 to 12 small holes in the lid (to reduce fogging and overheating in the jar). The jars can be decorated or labelled with names, if desired, using indelible markers or paint.

   Insect Aspirator.   An insect aspirator is a useful suction device for collecting small insects from the ground, flowers, or other micro-habitats. A professional aspirator is made out of a tall, narrow vial, rubber stopper, piece of 1/4" rubber hose, and a tiny screen. A simple children's version can be made from an empty film canister, two soda straws (with flexible necks), and a 1 inch square piece of pantyhose material (or similar porous cloth). Large numbers of empty film canisters can usually be obtained from most camera shops at no cost - just ask! Assembly of the aspirator is quite simple. (1) The holes in the film canister lid can be made with an ordinary paper punch; (2) Insert one of the straws into a hole with the long section of the straw above the lid (and outside of the canister). Insert the other straw in the opposite way, with the short section above the lid (and outside of the canister); (4) Cover the bottom end of this second straw with a small swatch of cloth, using glue, elastic band, or tape to hold it securely in place.

   To operate the aspirator you inhale on the short section of straw (the one with the cloth), which draws insects into the container. The cloth at the end of the straw keeps the insects from getting into your mouth! **NEVER put any alcohol of other chemicals (like those used in killing jars) in an aspirator!!** After aspirating is finished, transfer the insects from the aspirator to a killing jar, container of alcohol, or freezer, to kill any specimens you are going to keep for a collection.

   Insect Extractor. An "Insect Extractor" (known as a Berlese Funnel to entomologists) is used to extract and observe the incredible variety of tiny arthropods that live in soil, humus, and rotting wood. A simple, but effective, "insect extractor" can be easily made from a plastic two or three liter sodapop bottle.

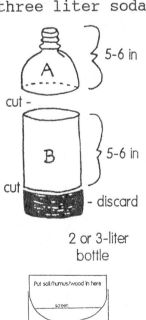

2 or 3-liter
bottle

   In addition to the bottle, a 6-8" square piece of screening (1/8 to 1/4" mesh, like that used for gutter screens) and a small plastic container (ie, film can, or bottle bottom) will be needed. A sharp knife or razorblade is used to cut the bottle into pieces. Construction, assembly, and use are as follows: (1) Cut the bottle as illustrated; (2) Cut a circular piece of screen so that it fits into the neck of the bottle, about 2" from the spout; (3) Invert part "A" (bottle top) and insert into top of part "B" (bottle middle); (4) Place circular screen into neck of bottle; (5) Place A/B assembly over the specimen receptacle (film can/jar lid), which has been filled with a preservative (alcohol or 50/50 water and antifreeze mixture); (6) Place loosely arranged handfuls of soil, leaf litter, humus, or rotten wood into the funnel and onto the screen. The screen should keep the mouth of the bottle from becoming clogged. As the material in the funnel begins to dry out, the hidden arthropods move downward until they finally fall out the bottom and tumble into the container filled with preservative. A light bulb (no greater than 60 watts) suspended over the funnel will speed up the drying process and the critter extraction rate.

For more information and ideas on making insect collecting equipment, see "A Beginner's Guide to Observing and Collecting Insects" by Gary A. Dunn (Young Entomologists' Society, Lansing, MI. 1994.).

INSECT COLLECTIONS

The best kind of insect collection for a child to make first is one of any kind of insect he/she can catch, anywhere they happen to be. After all, insects occur practically everywhere. To make a basic insect collection children will need a minimal amount of equipment, much of which costs very little or can be improvised from household materials. Essential equipment includes a net, collection jars, insect pins, spreading board (for butterflies and moths), insect labels (plain paper will do) and a fine point pen. Instructions for making these can be found in a number of beginning entomology books, such as "A Beginner's Guide to Observing and Collecting Insects" by Gary A. Dunn (Young Entomologists' Society, Lansing, MI. 1994.). Also, the Young Entomologists' Society has a variety of low cost equipment and supplies for sale by mailorder (write for a catalog).

After the children have mastered the basic insect collecting skills (hand collecting and insect net), they may want to try some innovative techniques that will help them collect a greater diversity of insects. Water-dwelling insects can be collected by aquatic techniques such as dip netting, treading, and emergence traps. Terrestrial or ground-dwelling insects, many of which are active only at night, can be collected using equipment such as a pitfall trap, pan trap, Berlese funnel, aspirator, headlamp, and emergence trap, and techniques such as sifting, flotation method, and baiting. The collection of aerial (flying) insects is not restricted to the use of nets. A large number of different flying insects can be captured with windowpane traps, Malaise traps, bait traps, and light traps. Plant-associated and arboreal insects may reside on or within a plant - the roots, wood, stems, twigs, leaves or fruits. To collect these insects, beating sheets and trays, aspirators, separator boxes, and emergence traps can be used. Animal-associated, or ectoparasitic, insects live on the exterior of a host. Extraction and animal nest collection techniques can be used to collect these types of insects. Detailed information on all of this collecting techniques can be found in "A Beginner's Guide to Observing and Collecting Insects" by Gary A. Dunn (Young Entomologists' Society, Lansing, MI. 1994.).

Whenever insects are collected (by any method), the date and where it was caught should be recorded so that the specimen becomes a valuable piece of scientific information. After the specimens are preserved this information will be written on a small label to accompany the specimen.

In addition to a general insect collection, there are other types of collections that can be make although these may be suitable for older, more experinced youth). For example, you can make a collection of representative adult insects from only the local area. You may also make a collection of insect eggs, larvae, pupae (rather than adult insects); or, you can make a collection of a special group of insects (by order, family or habitat), or other arthropod groups).

PRESERVING AND MOUNTING INSECTS FOR A COLLECTION

If you plan on keeping the insects you catch, they must be properly preserved and mounted. The use of proper preservation techniques will assure any collection efforts are not wasted and that the specimens will last for many years. Proper storage and care of a collection can make it last for a hundred years or more! Some of these techniques do require some manual dexterity, and practice will be required for most children. Have a child who has perfected a specific mounting technique (wing spreading, pinning with paper points, etc.) demonstrate the proper way to mount to the rest of the group. Insect pins can be obtained from college bookstores, biological supply houses, or the Young Entomologists' Society (send for a free catalog).

Here are some collection preparation tips to keep in mind:
(1) Whenever possible, insects must be mounted when fresh. Otherwise they may dry out and crumble when handled or pinned. Hard-bodied insects are usually preserved by dry mounting; soft-bodied insects are usually preserved in alcohol.
(2) If you must delay mounting insects, they can be stored temporarily in a refrigerator for up to a week to retain their suppleness. Specimens can be indefinitely stored if you put them in an air-tight container and put them in the freezer instead of the refrigerator. Many hard-bodied (adult) insects can also be temporarily stored in alcohol with satisfactory results. They can also be indefinitely stored in paper triangles, glassine envelopes, or layered between tissue paper in small boxes, but they will need to be relaxed before mounting.
(3) Insects are pinned through the thorax (the middle part of the insect body). Some variation occurs in the many groups of insects as to where they should be pinned. Consult any insect field guide, introductory entomology book, or basic entomology manual for specific instructions.
(4) The wings of butterflies and moths (and occasionally other insects with large wings) must be held down on a spreading board with paper strips and pins until the specimen is dry. This is a somewhat tricky task to learn and requires practice and patience!
(5) Specimens too small to pin should be mounted on small triangular points cut from index cards. Small soft-bodied insects should not be pinned or pointed at all, but should be preserved in small vials with alcohol.

Skills to Practice
(1) Have the children collect a few insects and practice the proper pinning of adult insect specimens, including the spreading of Lepidoptera, and pointing. See "A Beginner's Guide to Observing and Collecting Insects" by Gary A. Dunn (Young Entomologists' Society, Lansing, MI. 1994.), or other entomology reference for specific guidelines. Allow some insect specimens to dry out so that the children can compare mounting dried out insects with freshly killed insects.
(2) Have the children preserve representative soft-bodied adult insects and immatures (nymphs, naiads and larvae) in alcohol.

LABELING, STORING AND DISPLAYING COLLECTIONS

Once the insects are properly mounted, they should be labeled with the following information: location, date of capture, and name of collector(s). While it is not the most glamorous part of making an insect collection, it is the most important! Having insects accurately labeled and neatly displayed increases both the scientific and aesthetic value of a collection. Have the children practice properly labeling insects. Encourage them to share tips for making attractive labels.

Hopefully the children can construct or acquire their own collection boxes for storing their specimens. Insect collections must be properly stored in order to protect them from jarring and vibration, bright light (fading), dust, mold and dampness, and pests (dermestid beetles). Collections should be kept in a dark, dry, cool location. You may need to protect the collection from pests and fungi by using a fumigant and by avoiding moist, humid conditions.

You may want to arrange a visit to a large entomological (insect) collection at a University, science museum, or nature center to see how they care for their insect specimens. Call or write to make arrangements before you stop by to visit the collection. Most curators would be very happy to show you "their" collection if you give them time to prepare for your visit.

References

A Beginner's Guide to Observing and Collecting Insects. Gary A. Dunn. Young Entomologists' Society. Lansing, MI. 1994.
A Field Guide to the Insects. Donald J. Borror and Richard E. White. Houghton Mifflin, Boston. 1970.
Entomology: Real Kids/Real Science. Ellen Doris. Thames and Hudson, NY. 1993.
Insect Life. A Field Manual for the Amateur Naturalist. Ross Arnett and Richard Jacques. Prentice-Hall. 1985.
The Young Scientist Investigates Pond Life. Terry Jennings. Childrens' Press, Chicago. 1985.
The Young Scientist Investigates Small Garden Animals. Terry Jennings. Childrens' Press, Chicago. 1982.
The Practical Entomologist. Rick Imes. Simon and Schuster, NY. 1992.

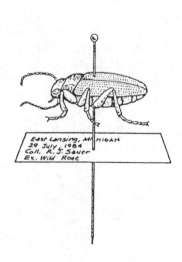

KEEPING AND REARING INSECTS

By caring for live insects children will have a chance to observe insect life cycles and other life processes under somewhat controlled conditions. By studying live insects, children can learn how insects breathe, feed, grow, behave, communicate, move, and reproduce. Reared insects may also provide valuable insight into ecological concepts such as symbiosis, competition, carry capacities, influence of environmental conditions, dispersal, and evolution.

Rearing activities can also help children develop responsibility and increase their ability to follow directions. In many cases the children can take an active role in planning and constructing mini-habitats for live insects and other arthropods. While this participation will greatly enhance the learning experience, be sure to place the mini-habitats where children can easily observe the creatures at frequent intervals. Also, be sure to provide tools to aid in observation and associated reference books. Monitor the children's interaction with the animals and provide additional guidance, project ideas, references, or tools as needed to keep up with their expanding investigations. After the mini-habitats are in use, a posted calendar or "duty roster" helps the children remember their responsibilities for feeding, watering, and caring for the live insects.

If an animal dies, be honest with the children and let them know what happened. Above all answer their questions as honestly as you can and don't make the death of an animal even more mysterious by disposing of the dead animal when they aren't around. Some children may need your support and understanding to express their feelings.

Insects that can be easily kept in the classroom include aquatic insects, house and field crickets, grasshoppers, giant cockroaches (Blaberus), hissing cockroaches (Gromphadorhina), praying mantises, walkingsticks, earwigs, termites, milkweed bugs, ground beetles, mealworms, flour beetles, ladybird beetles, bess beetles, wax moths, many butterflies and moths (painted ladies and silk moths), fruit flies, mosquitoes, and ants. Many other native insects can be reared if the natural habitat of the species can be reasonably duplicated in the classroom.

Live insect cultures can be obtained by purchasing insects from biological supply companies and pet shops, or by collecting them on your own. By gathering their own live insects, children will better understand the habitat and natural conditions of the species they are raising.

The children can make their own bug cage from two empty tuna/cat food cans, a bottle cap, a piece of screening (6" x 12"), a twig, a half cup of plaster of Paris, and a little water. Start by removing the labels and cleaning the cans. Next, paint or decorate the outside of the cans if

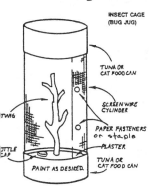

INSECT CAGE (BUG JUG)

TUNA OR CAT FOOD CAN

SCREEN WIRE CYLINDER

PAPER FASTENERS or staple

PLASTER

TUNA OR CAT FOOD CAN

TWIG

BOTTLE CAP

PAINT AS DESIRED.

desired. Study the picture of the completed bug cage to familiarize yourself with how it's put together. Place the 1/2 cup of plaster of Paris into one of the cans (more of you're using a larger can!), and slowly add small amounts of water. Mix the plaster until it is smooth and pudding-like. Set the bottle cap (water dish) and twig into the plaster. Roll the screen into a tube and and push it down into the plaster next to the edge of the can. You may need to push some of the wet plaster up against the screen and the edge of the can. There should be at least an inch of overlap in the screen; you can staple, fasten, or glue the overlapped area together, if needed. Set the cage in a warm, dry place so the plaster can harden. The second can is the lid. It slips down over the top of the cage, and can be removed to put insects in or to take them out. Conduct a field trip for the children to collect live insects followed by a session for them to set up the proper type of habitat for rearing their insects.

When keeping insects in captivity for a few days keep the following points in mind: (1) keep containers with insects out of the direct sun; (2) keep insects at room temperature, or slightly warmer (but not too hot); (3) keep insects in separate containers (unless you're studying life cycle or predation); (4) supply a little moisture (by sponge, wick, or shallow dish); (5) provide crumpled paper toweling (or similar material) for hiding/resting places, and (6) avoid and/or limit use of potentially toxic cleaning chemicals in the classroom. If you plan on keeping live insects for extended periods of time, you will need to read up on the habitat, environment, and other needs of the insect(s). Complete instructions for rearing 60 insects and other arthropods can be found in "Caring for Insect Livestock: An Insect Rearing Manual" by Gary A. Dunn (Young Entomologists' Society, Lansing, MI. 1993.).

If several children, or the entire group, are rearing live insects, arrange to have them display your groups' "insect zoo" at a school event, fair, nature center, or mall show.

REFERENCES: INSECT REARING INFORMATION

Adventures with Insects. Richard Headstrom. Dover Publications, New York. 1982.

Caring for Insect Livestock: An Insect Rearing Manual. Gary A. Dunn. Young Entomologists' Society, Lansing, MI. 1993.

Carolina Arthropods Manual. Anonymous. Carolina Biological Supply Co., Burlington, NC. 1982.

Critters in the Classroom. Robert W. Smith. Instructional Fair, Grand Rapids, MI. 1987.

How to Raise Butterflies. E. Jaedecker Norsgaard. Dodd, Mead and Co., New York. 1988.

How to Raise the Monarch Butterfly. Sally Spooner. Spooner Pub, Lakeville, MA. 1987.

Insect Life Cycle Studies. Gary A. Dunn. Michigan State Univ. Coop. Extension Service, 4-H 1406. 1988.

Insects Pets: Catching and Caring for Them. Carla Stevens. Greenwillow, New York. 1978.

Insect Zoo. How to Collect and Care for Animals. Constance Ewbank. Walker and Co., New York. 1973.

Keeping and Breeding Butterflies and Other Exotica. J.L.S. Stone. Sterling Publ., NY. 1992.

Keeping Minibeasts: Beetles. Barrie Watts. Silver Burdett, Morristown, NJ. 1989

Keeping Minibeasts: Butterflies and Moths. Barrie Watts. Silver Burdett, Morristown, NJ. 1991

Keeping Minibeasts: Caterpillars. Barrie Watts. Silver Burdett, Morristown, NJ. 1989

Keeping Minibeasts: Grasshoppers and Crickets. Barrie Watts. Silver Burdett, Morristown, NJ. 1991

Keeping Minibeasts: Ladybugs. Barrie Watts. Silver Burdett, Morristown, NJ. 1990.

Keeping Minibeasts: Stick Insects. Barrie Watts. Silver Burdett, Morristown, NJ. 1991.

Pets in a Jar. Seymour Simon. Viking Press, New York. 1987.

When a Pet Dies. Fred Rogers. G.P. Putnam's Sons. New York. 1988.

You Can Make an Insect Zoo. Roberta H. Roberts. Children's Press, Chicago. 1974.

MISCELLANEOUS TEACHING IDEAS

T-Shirts that Teach. A wide variety of colorful, educational insect T-shirts are available from many sources, including the Young Entomologists' Society. These shirts feature information on insect classification, insect groups, insects by habitat, life cycles, alphabets, insect "champions", and more. Wearing T-shirts with educational information on insects can be an innovative, fun way to get your point across!

Special Book Formats. Some insect books are available in "big book" format. These books, of course, are specially designed to be shared by a group of 6 to 10 children. When these books are used, the whole group can hear and see the story, and share in the reading experience.

If you work with children that don't read yet, collect books with matching cassette tapes. The audible beeps enable children to turn the pages at the right time and to "read" along. You might even want to make your own tape recording to go along with some of your favorite insect books that aren't commercially available on tape. They don't need to be elaborate studio productions (which probably don't impress the children anyway). For a little variety, you might want to enlist some volunteer narrators, possibly a local celebrity or TV/radio personality.

In recent years the release of insect books with 3-dimensional, pop-up figures has been on the increase. These books are unique in that they provide children with a more 3-dimensional view of the insect world. The trade off is that the books are often rather delicate and do not stand up well to use by large numbers of children. See the list of pop-up books on page 32.

FUN ACTIVITIES

The possibilities for fun activities with an insect theme are nearly limitless, and describing all of them is beyond the scope of this book. If you seek information on activities and projects (games, crafts, etc.) for young insect enthusiasts, you will find directions for more than 100 activities in "Organizing Bug Days and Insect Fairs" (published by the Young Entomologists' Society, 1994.). You will find this manual a valuable supplement to this book. Additional activities ideas may be found in some of the references cited on pages 42 through 44.

FINDING NEW TEACHING RESOURCES

The search for new insect teaching resources can reward you with the discovery of many exciting materials. Your search can be much less time consuming and more productive if you use "The Insect Study Sourcebook" by Gary A. Dunn (Young Entomologists' Society. 1994.). This resource guide with direct you to the individuals, businesses, and organizations that offer products and services for insect enthusiasts.

The "best of the best" in insect teaching resources is also available for purchase from the Young Entomologists' Society. Your purchase of materials from the Society not only makes your teaching job easier, but also supports the not-for-profit educational programs of the Young Entomologists' Society. Send for a free catalog.

INSECT STUDY ACROSS THE CURRICULUM

Integrating Insect Studies into the Curriculum

The study of insects should be an integral part of all creative science programs. Any educational experience, especially science, can be greatly enhanced by making it interdisciplinary. Many students who do not like science, but like other subjects, can be "turned on" to science merely by slipping it into other subjects. The opposite is true for children who excel in science, but see it as totally separate from other subject areas. Of course, nothing could be farther from the truth, because all scientists need to be able to read, write, problem-solve, and interact with other people on a regular basis.

Science and insect studies can help develop many useful skills, like observing, identifying, classifying, measuring, sequencing/ordering, interpreting data, formulating hypotheses, predicting outcomes, critical-thinking (problem solving), and communicating results and conclusions.

I strongly recommend that you use insect studies and activities as a way to enhance other subject areas and to promote creativity. For example, insect studies can be incorporated into child development and physical education (coordination and motor skill development through games and races; edible insects), writing (recording information; giving directions; reporting information; creative stories/poems to entertain), reading (fiction or nonfiction books about insects), art (draw, sculpt, and photograph insects or children participating in insect projects), performing arts (dance and music about insects), social studies (economics, insects that affected human history, insect folklore, civics, and geography), mathematics (counting, measuring, graphing, computations, word problems, sequencing, symmetry, and geometry), and science (experimentation and the scientific method, biology and life cycles, ecology, earth science, space exploration, physics, and chemistry).

Using Literature to Teach Children

Literature, including story books, represents a storehouse of knowledge and experience that informs and instructs as it entertains. It brings scientific facts together in a holistic manner, disproving the idea that science is a collection of isolated data, facts, statistics, and concepts.

According to Kenneth E. Barber (Washington State University Extension Service), "children like stories because they are fun, active, personal, and exciting experiences. Children have fun with the words and pictures, as well as with the person reading the story. Using books with children who aren't able to read yet has another advantage. Seeing you use books is an excellent experience for them. It helps them understand the value of books. They learn that everyone, even adults, need the help that books have to offer."

Children find enjoyment with the ideas that they hear and see because their minds are open and growing. Stories can help them recreate the world they know, and help them understand and enjoy it more fully. A story can introduce children to new thoughts, experiences, information, and unfamiliar events. Reading a story can be one part of an overall strategy for introducing a value, idea, or information to children. Stories expose children to rich and varied use of language and enrich their creative capacities. They also provide exposure to people, places, and things that they may never be able to see or have personal contact with. In short, the storyline in these books helps children to understand and remember important scientific concepts, probably to a greater extent than when the same information is presented in a science text book!

Good stories can also answer children's questions. At some time in their lives, all children are faced with issues such as acceptance, rejection, siblings, death, anger, and selfworth. A story can respond to those concerns and give children a sense of hope and mastery over life's challenges.

The books (both fiction and nonfiction) listed on the following pages can be used directly or indirectly to help children learn and practice important educational skills, using the high-appeal insect theme. When integrated into your overall curriculum the educational experience is greatly enhanced and your lessons will have greater impact. Your librarian, or the staff at the Young Entomologists' Society, would be glad to help you with information on the availability of these and other useful books.

These are just a few suggestions to get you started.... Have fun!

INSECT BIG BOOKS

Some insect books are available in "big book" format. These books, of course, are specially designed to be shared by a group of 6 to 10 children. When these books are used, the whole group can hear and see the story, and share in the reading experience.

Bugs! Patricia and Frederick McKissack. Childrens Press. Chicago. 1988.
It's a Good Thing There Are Insects. Allan Fowler. Childrens Press. Chicago. 1990.
Fascinating Insects. Anonymous. Educational Insights. Dominguez Hills, CA. 1992.
Butterflies and Moths. Christine Butterworth. Steck-Vaughn Co. Austin, TX. 1993?.
Butterfly and Caterpillar (Stopwatch Book). Barrie Watts. Silver Burdett Press. Englewood Cliffs, NJ. 1986.
Dragonfly (Stopwatch Book). Barrie Watts. Silver Burdett Press. Englewood Cliffs, NJ. 1988.
Honeybee (Stopwatch Book). Barrie Watts. Silver Burdett Press. Englewood Cliffs, NJ. 1989.
Ladybug (Stopwatch Book). Barrie Watts. Silver Burdett Press. Englewood Cliffs, NJ. 1987.
Moth (Stopwatch Book). Barrie Watts. Silver Burdett Press. Englewood Cliffs, NJ. 1990.
Which Way Now? J. Croser and M. Quick. Educational Insights. Dominguez Hills, CA. 1987.
Why Mosquitoes Buzz in People's Ears. Verna Aardema. Dial Press. New York. 1975.

BOOKS WITH CASSETTES

If you work with children who can't read on their own yet, collect books with matching cassette tapes. The audible beeps enable children to turn the pages at the right time and to "read" along. You might even want to make your own tape recording to go along with some of your favorite insect books that aren't commercially available on tape. They don't need to be elaborate studio productions (which probably don't impress the children anyway). For a little variety, you might want to enlist some volunteer narrators.

Boogie Woogie Bugs Activity Book. Don Cooper. Random House. New York. 1989.

I Can Read About Insects. Deborah Merrians. Troll Associates. Mahwah, NJ. 1977.

Insects. Keith Brandt. Troll Associates. Mahwah, NJ. 1985.

Life Cycle of the Butterfly. Paula Hogan. Steck-Vaughn Co. Austin, TX. 1979.

Which Way Now? J. Croser and M. Quick. Educational Insights. Dominguez Hills, CA. 1987.

STORY BOOKS WITH INSECT CHARACTERS

The following story books can be used to supplement and enhance your teaching on insects. When used in combination with insect puppets, these stories can have greater impact (especially with young insect enthusiasts). Many insect characters are available from the Young Entomologists' Society, including ant, caterpillar/butterfly, cockroach, firefly, dragonfly, grasshopper, house fly, ladybug, and monarch butterfly.

Additional book titles can be found in the section on books with insect folktales and multicultural themes (pages 38 and 39).

Amanda's Butterfly. Nick Butterworth. Delacorte Press. New York. 1991.

The Bee. Lisa Campbell Ernst. Lothrup, Lee & Shepard. New York. 1986.

The Bee Sneeze. Beverly Keller. Coward, McCann & Geoghegan. New York. 1982.

Beetles Toasted Lightly. Phyllis Naylor. Atheneum. New York. 1987.

Billy's Beetle. Mick Inkpen. Gulliver/HBJ. New York. 1991.

The Cabbage Moth and the Shamrock. Ethel Marbach. Simon and Schuster. New York. 1978.

The Case of the Anteater's Missing Lunch. Jeffrey Nelson. Silver Burdett Press. Columbus, OH. 1990.

Charlie Cricket. Emma George. Modern Publishing Co. New York. 1989.

Down the River without a Paddle. Robert & Claire Wiest. Childrens Press. Chicago. 1973.

A Firefly Named Torchy. Bernard Waber. Houghton Mifflin. Boston. 1970.

Grasshopper on the Road. Arnold Lobel. Harper & Row. New York. 1978.

A House of Leaves. Kiyoshi Soya. Philomel. New York. 1986.

I Love to Eat Bugs! John Strejan. Price Stern Sloan. Los Angeles. 1992.

I Was Born in a Tree and Raised by Bees. Jim Arnosky. Bradbury Press. Scarsdale, NY. 1988.

Lady Bugatti. Joyce Maxner. Lothrup, Lee & Shepard. New York. 1990.

Ladybug, Ladybug. Ruth Brown. E.P. Dutton. New York. 1988.

Maggie and the Pirate. Ezra J. Keats. Macmillan. New York. 1987.

Nicolas Cricket. Joyce Maxner. Harper & Row. New York. 1989.

No Fleas, Please! Michael Pellowski. Troll Assoc. Mahwah, NJ. 1986.

Old Black Fly. Jim Aylesworth. Henry Holt and Co. New York. 1992.

Perfect Percy. Bonnie Pryor. Simon & Schuster. New York. 1988.

Rilloby-rill. Sir John Newbolt. O'Hara. UK. 1973.

Sam's Sandwich. David Pelham. E.P. Dutton. New York. 1990.

Sir Small and the Dragonfly. Jane O'Connor. Random House. New York. 1988.

Step By Step. Diane Wolkstein. Morrow Junior Books. New York. 1994.

Two Bad Ants. Christopher Van Allsburg. Houghton Mifflin. Boston. 1988.

INFORMATIVE "BUG" BOOKS WITH FICTIONAL CHARACTERS

The following books can be used to teach children a variety of important information on insects. When used in combination with insect puppets or giant rubber "bugs", your lessons can have greater impact (especially with young insect enthusiasts). The puppets can be used to teach many aspects of insect biology (life cycles and metamorphosis) and behavior (feeding, mating, and defense). Many arthropod characters are available from the Young Entomologists' Society, including an ant, caterpillar/butterfly, cockroach, firefly, dragonfly, grasshopper, house fly, ladybug, and monarch butterfly. Try using them to illustrate some of the stories listed below.

All Upon a Sidewalk. Jean Craighead George. E.P. Dutton. New York. 1974.

The Ants Go Marching. Berniece Freshet. Scribner's Sons. NY. 1973.

Biography of a Bee. Naida Dickson. Lerner Publications. Minneapolis, MN. 1974.

Butterflies and Moths. Nature stories for Children. Barbara Batulla. Hyperion Press. Winnipeg. 1983.

The Butterfly. A. Delaney. Crown Publishers. New York. 1977.

Buzz, Buzz, Buzz. Byron Barton. Macmillan Publ. New York. 1973.

The Carpenter Bee. Ross E. Hutchins. Addison-Wesley. Reading, MA. 1972.

The Caterpillar and the Polliwog. Jack Kent. Prentice-Hall. New York. 1982.

Caterpillar Caterpillar Vivian French. Candlewick Press. Cambridge, MA. 1993.

The Caterpillar Who Turned into a Butterfly. Anonymous. Simon and Schuster. New York. 1980.

Collecting Bugs and Things. Julia Spencer Moutran. Price Stern Sloan. Los Angeles. 1988.

Fireflies. Julie Brinkloe. MacMillan. New York. 1985.

The Great Bug Hunt. Bonnie Dobkin. Childrens Press. Chicago. 1993.

The Honey Bee and the Robber. Eric Carle. Philomel. New York. 1985.

If I Were an Ant. Amy Moses. Childrens Press. Chicago. 1992.

Insects. Nature Stories for Children. Barbara Batulla. Hyperion Press. Winnipeg. 1983.

Life of a Queen. Collette Portal. Braziller, Inc. New York. 1964.

Look Closer. Brian & Rebecca Wildsmith. HBJ. New York. 1993.

McBroom's Ear. Albert Sidney Fleishman. William Norton & Co. New York. 1969.

Peek-a-Bug. Jerry Smath. Random House. New York. 1990.

The Pet in the Jar. Judy Stang. Golden Press. Racine, WI. 1975.

The Travels of Monarch X. Ross E. Hutchins. Rand McNally. New York. 1969.

The Very Hungry Caterpillar. Eric Carle. Philomel Books. New York. 1979.

Where Does the Butterfly Go When it Rains? May Garelick. Scholastic Inc. New York. 1961.

INSECT BOOKS AND CHILD DEVELOPMENT

Manipulatives

Books are not just for looking any more! Many recently published insect books have special manipulative activities (holes, tabs, wheels, sound devices, 3-D pop-ups, etc.) that intrigue children and help them refine their motor skills while learning about insects.

In recent years the release of insect books with 3-dimensional, pop-up figures has been on the increase. These books are unique in that they provide children with a more 3-dimensional view of the insect world. The trade off is that the books are often rather delicate and do not stand up well to use by large numbers of children.

Ant. David Hawcock and Lee Montgomery. Random House. New York. 1994.
Bee. David Hawcock and Lee Montgomery. Random House. New York. 1994.
The Bee. Beth B. Norden. Stewart, Tabori & Chang. New York. 1991.
The Beetle. Maria Mudd. Stewart, Tabori & Chang. New York. 1992.
The Butterfly. Maria Mudd. Stewart, Tabori & Chang. New York. 1991.
Butterfly Match and Patch. Opal Dunn. Dell Publ. New York. 1991.
Frightful Winged Creatures. Ken Hoy. Ideals Publ. Co. Nashville, TN. 1993.
If at First You Do Not See. Ruth Brown. Henry Holt and Co. New York. 1982.
Insects: A Close-up Look. Macmillan Publishing Co. New York. 1984.
Ladybug on the Move. Richard Fowler. Harcourt Brace. New York. 1993.
My Pop-Up Garden Friends. Rod Campbell. Macmillan Publishing Co. New York. 1992.
Peek-a-Bug. Jerry Smath. Random House. New York. 1990.
The Ultimate Bug Book. Luise Woelflein. Western Publ. Co. New York. 1993.

Color Recognition
Squiggly Wiggly's Surprise. Arnold Shapiro. Price Stern Sloan. Los Angeles. 1978.

Telling Time
The Ants Who Took Away Time. William Kotzwinkle. Doubleday. New York. 1978.
The Grouchy Ladybug. Eric Carle. Harper & Row. New York. 1977.

Directional Relationships
Which Way Now? J. Croser and M. Quick. Educational Insights. Dominguez Hills, CA. 1987.

Social Skills
The Ant and the Dove. Mary Lewis Wang. Children's Press. Chicago. 1989 [friendship]
The Ant and the Elephant. Bill Peet. Houghton-Mifflin. Boston. 1972. [helpfulness]
Bear Circus. William DuBois. Viking Press. NY. 1971. [helpfulness]
The Bee Tree. Patricia Polacco. Philomel Books. New York. 1993. [value of reading]
Best Bug to Be. Dolores Johnson. Macmillan. New York. 1992. [living with disappointment]
Blue Bug and the Bullies. Virginia Poulet. Children's Press. Chicago. 1971 [relationships]
Both Sides Now. Joni Mitchell. Scholastic. New York. 1992. [self esteem and change]
The Butterfly Hunt. Yoshi. Picture Book Studio. Saxonville, MA. 1990. [respecting living creatures]
The Butterfly Night of Old Brown Bear. Nicolas van Pallandt. Farrar, Strauss & Giroux. New York. [desires and expectations]
Charlie the Caterpillar. Dom DeLuise. Simon & Schuster. New York. 1993. [friendship and self esteem]
Effie. Beverley Allinson. Scholastic. New York. 1990. [unique

talents]
Fireflies! Julie Brinckloe. Aladdin Books. New York. 1985. [respect for living creatures]
Freddie the Fly. Charles Grodin. Random House. New York. 1993. [friendship and resourcefulness]
The Giant Jam Sandwich. John Vernon Lord. Houghton Mifflin. Boston. 1972. [ingenuity]
The Girl Who Loved Caterpillars. Jean Merrill. Philomel. New York. 1991. [self esteem and fulfillment]
The Gnats of Knotty Pine. Bill Peet. Houghton Mifflin. Boston. 1975. [teamwork and self esteem]
The Grouchy Ladybug. Eric Carle. Harper & Row. New York. 1977. [relationships and telling time]
I Wish I Were a Butterfly. James Howe. Harcourt Brace Jovanovich. San Diego. 1987. [self esteem]
John J. Plenty and Fiddler Dan. John Ciardi. Lippincott. Philadelphia. 1963. [preparedness]
Just a Little Bit. Ann Tompert. Houghton Mifflin. Boston. 1993. [each individual's contribution counts]
Ladybug and Dof and the Night Walk. Polly Berends. Random House. New York. 1980. [friendship]
Ladybug, Ladybug. Robert Kraus. Harper and Row, New York. 1957. [misunderstandings]
The Lamb and the Butterfly. Arnold Sundgard. Franklin Watts. New York. 1988. [individuality]
Lettie at the Pond. Anonymous. Ramboro Books. London. 1985. [cooperation]
Michael Bird-boy. Tomie dePaola. Prentice-Hall. New York. 1975. [ingenuity and environmental protection]
One Dragon to Another. Ned Delaney. Houghton-Mifflin. Boston. 1976. [individuality]
On the Wings of a Butterfly. Marilyn Maple. Parenting Press. 1993. [coping with a terminal disease]
Remember the Butterflies. Anna Hines. E.P. Dutton. New York. 1991. [death of a family member]
Sam and the Firefly. P.D. Eastman. Random House. New York. 1958. [consequences of disobeying]
Sloan and Philamina; Or, How to Make Friends with Your Lunch. Patti Stren. E.P. Dutton, New York. 1979. [friendship]
The Spelling Bee. Sharon Gordon. Troll Assoc. Mahwah, NJ. 1981. [spelling's importance]
The Spider and the Fly. Cathie Shuttleworth. Barron's. Toronto. 1987. [strangers]
The Very Quiet Cricket. Eric Carle. Philomel Books. New York. 1990. [self esteem]
When the Woods Hum. Joanne Ryder. Morrow. New York. 1991. [family traditions]
Why Mosquitoes Buzz in People's Ears; A West African Tale. Verna Aardema. Dial Press. New York. 1975. [consequences of telling lies]

INSECT BOOKS AND MATHEMATICS

Counting and Arithmatic Skills

The insects are the most abundant animals in the world, both in numbers of species and individuals, so it's appropriate that they should be used in teaching counting and math skills!

The Ants Go Marching. Berniece Freshet. Charles Scribner's Sons. New York. 1973.

Billions of Bugs. Harris Petie. Prentice-Hall. New York. 1975.

Bugs! Patricia and Frederick McKissack. Childrens Press. Chicago. 1988.

Count in the Dark with Glowworm. Anonymous. Random House. New York. 1985

Deep Down Underground. Oliver Dunrea. Macmillan Publishing Co. New York. 1993.

The Icky Bug Counting Book. Jerry Pallotta. Charlesbridge Publishing. Cambridge, MA. 1992.

Inch By Inch. Leo Lionni. Scholastic, Inc. New York. 1960.

One Green Mesquite Tree. Gisela Jernigan. Harbinger House. Tucson, AZ. 1992.

One Hundred Hungry Ants. Elinor Pinczes. Houghton-Mifflin. Boston. 1993.

INSECT BOOKS AND LANGUAGE ARTS

Writing About Insects. As you and the children observe and study insects you will begin to notice many small details about their activities. The need for children to describe what they see in the insect world will result in a rapidly increasing descriptive language.

As they become a little older they will see that all scientists, including entomologists, need to be able to communicate in writing. They need to be able to record their observations, to write descriptions of insects, to share information with other entomologists, to give instructions, to write letters and reports, and to express opinions and thoughts.

Becoming a good writer takes practice, and writing about insects can make it fun. Provide opportunities to practice writing by introducing children to the concept of keeping a nature (insect) journal in which they can record their observations, write creative stories, or express their thoughts and feelings about insects. If a special entomological guest visits or they go on a field trip, have them write thank you notes.

Insect Book Reports. Book reports aren't out of date, nor are they for fiction books only. To encourage children to thoroughly read insect nonfiction (fact) books you can assign a special book report and ask for an annotated list of "25 Important Facts" that they discovered in the book. Insist on at least one fact from every chapter, and to authenticate the fact have them list the chapter and page number where the fact can be found. In fact, to make this activity easier you might suggest that the children make notes (brief description of the fact, chapter and page number!) of significant facts they encounter while reading. Later, they can return to each reference and finalize their annotated list.

Your children can become published writers! The Young Entomologists' Society publishes articles, stories, poems, riddles, and jokes on insects and spiders from writers of all ages, including children. To have materials considered for publication in one of the Y.E.S. periodicals, send them to the Y.E.S. Editor, Young Entomologists' Society, 1915 Peggy Place, Lansing, MI 48910-2553.

Also, keep in mind that other forms of language blend with creative expression in the form of music, plays, and poems.

The Alphabet

ANTics! Cathi Hepworth. G.P. Putnam's Sons. New York. 1992.

The Icky Bug Alphabet Book. Jerry Pallotta. Charlesbridge Publishing. Cambridge, MA. 1986.
The Icky Bug Counting Book. Jerry Pallotta. Charlesbridge Publishing. Cambridge, MA. 1992. [it's alphabetic too!]
Old Black Fly. Jim Aylesworth. Henry Holt and Co. New York. 1992.

Vocabulary Skills
ANTics! Cathi Hepworth. G.P. Putnam's Sons. New York. 1992.

Poems
Insects make excellent subjects for poems, including specialized styles like haiku, cinquain, and diamonte.

All Upon a Stone. Jean Craighead George. Thomas Crowell. New York. 1971.
Because the Little Boy Went Ka-choo! Rosetta Stone. Random House. New York. 1971.
Bugs. Nancy Parker and J.R. Wright. William Morrow. New York. 1987.
Bugs: Poems. Mary Ann Hoberman. Viking Press. New York. 1976.
Butterflies Are Beautiful. Ruth F. Brin. Lerner Publications. Minneapolis, MN. 1974.
The Butterfly Collector. Naomi Lewis. Prentice-Hall. New York. 1979.
The Butterfly's Ball. William Roscoe. MacGraw-Hill. New York. 1967.
Cricket in the Thicket. Aileen Fisher. Charles Scribner's Sons, New York. 1963.
Demi's Secret Garden. Demi. Henry Holt and Co. New York. 1993.
Flit, Flutter and Fly. Lee Bennett Hopkins. Delacorte Press. New York. 1992.
The Great Bug Hunt. Bonnie Dobkin. Childrens Press. Chicago. 1993.
Hey Bug! And Other Poems About Little Things. Elizabeth Itze. American Heritage Press. New York. 1972.
If I Were a Cricket. Kazue Mizumura. Thomas Crowell Co. New York. 1973.
I Like Caterpillars. Gladys Conklin. Holiday House. New York. 1958.
Insect Appreciation Digest. Tom Turpin. Entomological Foundation. Lanham, MD. 1992.
Itsy Bitsy Beasties. Poems from Around the World. Michael Rosen. Carolrhoda Books. Minneapolis, MN. 1992.
Joyful Noise: Poems for Two Voices. Paul Fleishman. Harper/Collins. New York. 1988.
Ladybird Quickly. Juliet Kepes. Little, Brown and Co. Boston. 1964.
Never Say Ugh to a Bug. Norma Farber. Greenwillow. New York. 1979.
When It Comes to Bugs. Aileen Fisher. Harper & Row. New York. 1986.

Storytelling
Willie the Bug Man. Susan Klein. Oak Bluffs, MA. 1987. (audio cassette)

Riddles and Jokes
101 Bug Jokes. L. Eisenberg and K. Hall. Scholastic. New York. 1984.
102 Creepy, Crawly Bug Jokes. Ski Michaels. Troll Associates. Mahwah, NJ. 1992.
Buggy Riddles. K. Hall and L. Eisenberg. Dial Press. New York. 1986.
Creepy Crawly Critter Riddles. J.E. Bernstein and Paul Cohen. Albert Whitman Co. Niles, IL. 1992.

Foreign and Second Language Skills

Many insect books (both fiction and nonfiction) are now available in non-English versions that can help integrate foreign and second language skills with insect studies.

Animales de Jardin. Terry Jennings. CESNA, Madrid 1990.
Cuenta Los Insectos. Jerry Pallotta. Charlesbridge Publishing. Cambridge, MA. 1992.
De la Flor a la Miel. Gertrudis Zenzes. Fernandez editores. Mexico City, MEXICO. 1987.
Descubre Mariposas. Gary A. Dunn. Publications International. Lincolnwood, IL. 1992.
Dona Cigarra y Dona Hormiga. Jose Antonio Elgorriaga. LTO Enterprises. Phoenix. 1987.
El Misterio de Melodia. Diane and Bob Harvey. Beautiful America Publishing Co. 1993.
Insectos! Patricia and Frederick McKissack. Children's Press. Chicago, IL. 1988.
La Chenille Affamee Eric Carle. Putnam/Philomel. New York. 1992.
La coccinelle. Sylvaine Perols. Gallimand. Paris. 1989.
La Mariguita Malhumorada. Eric Carle. Harper/Collins. NY. 1992.
Las Mariposas (Como Son). David Cutts. Sistemas Tecnicos, Mexico City. 1988.
Le Livre des Insectes. Gaelan Du Chatent. Gallimand. Paris. 1990.
Los Insectos. L. Mound. Santillana Publ. Co. Compton, CA. 19??.
Melody's Mystery/El Misterio de Melodia. Diane and Bob Harvey. Beautiful America Publ. Co. 1993.
Que Beuno Que Haya Insectos! Alan Fowler. Childrens Press. Chicago. 1991.

INSECT BOOKS AND CREATIVE EXPRESSION

Insects have been, and continue to be, represented in many forms artistic expression, from simple crafts to the fine arts -- just look around! Insects have influenced the designers of toys, fabrics, wallpaper, pottery, sculpture, jewelry, and other forms of artistic expression. Look for examples in your local community.

In an educational setting, insects can be the subjects for a whole variety of art projects such as banners and flags, batik, block prints, computer art, decoupage, dried flower arrangements, face painting, greeting cards, jewelry, mobiles, needlecraft, photography, puppets, rubber stamp art, sculpture, silk screening, stencils, video and film-making, wood burning, and wood carving. Directions and materials for many types of creative and artistic projects can be found in the books listed below.

Your children can become published illustrators! The Young Entomologists' Society publishes drawings of insects and spiders from artists of all ages, including children. To have materials considered for publication in one of the Y.E.S. periodicals, send them to the Y.E.S. Editor, Young Entomologists' Society, 1915 Peggy Place, Lansing, MI 48910-2553.

Arts and Crafts

Animal Activities: Insects. Jan Ormesher. Judy/Instructo. Minneapolis, MN. 1987.
Bats, Bugs and Butterflies. A Book of Action Toys. S. Adams Sullivan, Little, Brown and Co. Boston. 1990.

Butterflies. A Colors of Nature Book. Malcolm White. Price Stern
     Sloan. Los Angeles, CA. 1989. [coloring book]
Butterflies of Eastern North America. A Coloring Album and Activity
     Book. Paul Opler. Roberts Rinehart Publ. Boulder, CO. 1989.
     [coloring book]
Butterflies of the American West. Paul Opler. Roberts Rinehart
     Publishers. Boulder, CO. 1988. [coloring book]
Butterflies Stained Glass Coloring Book. Ed Sibbett, Jr. Dover. New
     York. 1985.
Butterfly Iron-On Transfer Patterns. Barbara Christopher. Dover
     Publications. Mineola, NY. 1991.
Coloring Fun With Insects. Edwin King. Entomological Society of
     America. Lanham, MD. 1983. [coloring book]
Draw 50 Creepy Crawlies. Lee J. Ames. Doubleday. New York. 1991.
Exotic Butterflies Charted Designs. Jamie Rusek. Dover Publications.
     Mineola, NY. 1991.
If at First You Do Not See. Ruth Brown. Henry Holt and Co. New York.
     1982.
Insects. A Fact-filled Coloring Book. George Glenn, Jr. Running
     Press. Philadelphia, PA. 1991. [coloring book]
Insects. Peterson Field Guide Coloring Books. Robert M. Pyle and
     Kristin Kest. Houghton Mifflin Co. Boston, MA. 1993. [coloring
     book]
Monsters, Animals and Airplanes to Color, Cut and Fly. Richard Wagner.
     Price Stern Sloan. Los Angeles. 1989.
Paper Predators: Spider. D. Johnston and L. Mound. Dell Publishing,
     NY. 1992.
Seguy's Decorative Butterflies and Insects .... E.A. Seguy. Dover
     Publications. Mineola, NY. 1977.
When Clay Sings. Byrd Baylor. Charles Scribner's Sons. New York.
     1972. [insect art of ancient Native Americans]

Photography
     You've no doubt heard the old saying, "A picture is worth a thousand
words." Well, there is a lot of truth to this old saying, because many
insect activities can be documented for close study with photographs.
Photographs are important for documenting insect natural histories and
revealing details of structure or coloration, as well as recording your
investigations and activities. Photographing insects can also be an
alternative to collecting and killing them. In addition to the portrait
of the insect, a photo will also record information on the habitat, host
and food plants, and environmental conditions.
     The availability of relatively inexpensive, but sophisticated, video
camcorders has even made it possible to record insects in the act of being
themselves!

Hatch and Grow: Life Stories of Familiar Insects. Abeland-Schuman.
     London. 1967.
Insects Close Up. Univ. of California Press. Berkeley. 1953.
Insects: Hunters and Trappers. Ross E. Hutchins. Rand McNally. Skokie
     IL. 1957.

Music
     Insects have also been exalted through music, with famous and familiar
songs such as "Flight of the Bumble Bee", "Glowworm", "Shoo, Fly, Don't
Bother Me", and "Jimmy Crack Corn (The Blue Tail Fly)". Through songs you
and the children can learn many interesting facts about insects while
having fun with rhythm and rhyme. You may want to check out some of the
songbooks and cassette tapes mentioned below.

The Ants Go Marching One by One. Richard Bernal. Publications International. Lincolnwood, IL. 1993.
Butterfly (StorySongs). Ron Brown. Perfection Learning Corp. Logan, IA. 1991. (audio cassette)
A Creepy Crawly Songbook. Hiawyn, Oram, Carl Davis and Satoshi Kitamuri. Farrar, Strauss & Giroux. New York. 1993.
Boogie Woogie Bugs Activity Book. Don Cooper. Random House. New York. 1989.
BugPlay. M.N. Hapai and L.H. Burton. Addison-Wesley. Reading, MA. 1990.
Bugs, Beetles and Butterflies. Sharron Lucky. DLM Teaching Resources. Allen, TX. 1989.
Grandpa Art: Insects. Arthur Custer. Sun Group. New York. 1992. (audio cassette)
Insects, Bugs and Squiggly Things. Jane Murphy. Kimbo. Long Branch, NJ. 1993. (audio cassette)
London Bridge Is Falling Down. Richard Bernal. Publications International. Lincolnwood, IL. 1993.
Sing-along Science: Insects. Linda Penn and Kerry Clark. Young Entomologists' Society, Lansing. 1992. (audio cassette tape)
Songs About Metamorphosis. Ron Brown. Perfection Learning Corp. Logan, IA. 1991. (audio cassette tape)

INSECT BOOKS AND SOCIAL STUDIES

Geography
There is no land mass on this earth that is not occupied by members of the insect world. Their varied distributions and migrations can be the basis for studying geography, both past and present.

The Great Butterfly Chase. R.W.N. Prior. Bradbury Press. New York. 1993.
Giants of the Insect World. Geoffrey T. Williams. Price Stern Sloan. Los Angeles. 1991.

Folklore and Multicultural Themes
People from many lands and from all times have been fascinated by the activities and abilities of insects. This has led to the establishment of many interesting sayings, beliefs, and folktales around the world. Understanding the origins of folklore can teach us a lot about ourselves and the people of other cultures.

The Butterfly Boy. Laurence Yep. Farrar, Strauss & Giroux. New York. 1993.
Chin Ling, the Chinese Cricket. Alison Stilwell. Stilwell Studios. 1981.
Dragonfly's Tale. Kristina Rodanas. Clarion Books. New York. 1992.
The Fireflies. Max Bollinger. Antheneum Press. New York. 1970. [A Czechoslovakian folktale of fireflies and family life]
Fireflies in the Night. Judy Hawes. Thomas Crowell. New York. 1963.
Fire Race: A Karuk Coyote Tale. Jonathan London. Chronicle Books. San Francisco. 1993.
The Girl Who Loved Caterpillars. Jean Merrill. Philomel. NY. 1991.
The Golden Butterfly. Marta Osario. Silver Burdett Press. Englewood Cliffs, NJ. 1985.
Grasshopper to the Rescue: A Georgian Tale. Bonnie Carey. William Morrow and Co. New York. 1979.

The Honeyhunters. Francesca Martin. Candlewick Press. Cambridge MA.
    1992.
I Can Squash Elephants: A Masai Tale About Monsters. Malcolm Carrick.
    Viking Press. New York. 1978.
Insect Fact and Folklore. Lucy Clausen. Collier. New York. 1954.
Itsy-Bitsy Beasties. Poems From Around the World. Michael Rosen.
    Carolrhoda Books. Minneapolis, MN. 1992.
Ladybug, Ladybug, Fly Away Home. Judy Hawes. Thomas Crowell Co. New
    York. 1967.
The Land of Right Up and Down. Eva-Lis Wuorio. World Publ. New York.
    1964.
Leave That Cricket Be, Alan Lee. Barbara Ann Porte. 1993.
A Story, A Story. Gail E. Haley. Atheneum. New York. 1970.
That's What It Is! Ruth M. Jaynes. Bowman. 1968. [Mexican-American
    folktales about insects]
When Clay Sings. Byrd Baylor. Charles Scribner's Sons. New York.
    1972. [insect art of ancient Native Americans]
Who's in Rabbits House? Verna Aardema. Dial Press. New York. 1977.
Why Mosquitoes Buzz in People's Ears: A West African Tale. Verna
    Aardema. Dial Press. New York. 1975.

Human History
    As our greatest competitors, insects have had profound effects on
humankind ever since the emergence of man. They attack our bodies, our
livestock and crops, and consume our food and homes. Some have even
changed the course of human history!

First to Fly. Robert R. Moulton. Lerner Publishing Co. Minneapolis,
    MN. 1983.
Insect Attack. Christopher Lampton. Millbrook Press. Brookfield, CT.
    1992.
Insects, Creeping Conquerors and Human History Carson Ritchie. Thomas
    Nelson Co. New York. 1979.
Killers: Insects and Spiders. Philip Steele. Julian Messner.
    Englewood Cliffs, NJ. 1991.
The Little Killer: Fleas, Lice, Mosquitoes. Wyatt Blassingame. G. P.
    Putnam's Sons. New York. 1975.
The Mosquito: Its Life, Activities and Impact on Human Affairs. W.D.
    Gillet. Doubleday. New York. 1972.
Rats, Lice and History. Hans Zinsser. Bantam Books. New York. 1960.

Human Nutrition and Insects
    It is well known that insects are the major source of nourishment for
animals like birds, fish, reptiles, amphibians, and many small mammals.
It is less well known that insects have nourished humans as well, and
could provide a viable solution to the critical food shortages experienced
in many parts of the world. Insects, which are high in protein, have been
a valuable dietary supplement in many human cultures past and present.

Beetles Toasted Lightly. Phyllis Naylor. Atheneum. New York. 1987.
Butterflies in My Stomach. Ronald Taylor. Woodbridge Press. Santa
    Barbara, CA. 1975.
Entertaining with Insects. Or, The Original Guide to Insect Cookery.
    Ronald Taylor. Woodbridge Press. Santa Barbara, CA. 1976

A Day in the Life of a Beekeeper. Troll Associates. P. Michaels and
    J. Tropea. Mahwah, NJ. 1991.
Insect Potporri: Adventures in Entomology. Jean Adams. Sandhill Crane
    Press. Gainesville, FL. 1992.
The Pleasures of Entomology. Howard E. Evans. Smithsonian Institution
    Press. Washington, DC. 1985

FACT BOOKS (NONFICTION)

It is, of course, impractical to list all the insect books that are
available, but the following titles are among the very best. Many of the
following books will help relate the study of insects to other science
topics, like the scientific method, life cycles, ecology, and botany. For
additional information on insect books for youth, see "Buggy Books: A
Guide to Juvenile and Popular Books on Insects and their Relatives" by
Gary A. Dunn (Young Entomologists' Society, Lansing. 1990.) and the Y.E.S.
"Buggy Bookstore" catalog.

Amazing Beetles. John Still. A.A. Knopf, New York. 1991.
Ant. Andrienne Soutter-Perrot. American Education Publishing. 1993.
Ant Cities. Arthur Dorros. Harper Trophy, New York. 1987.
An Ant Colony. H. & A. Fischer-Nagel. Carolrhoda. Minneapolis. 1989.
Ants. Cynthia Overbeck. Lerner Publications. Minneapolis. 1982.
Ants (Life Story) Michael Chinery. Troll Associates. Mahwah, NJ.
    1990.
Aquatic Insects and How They Live. Robert McClung. William Morrow and
    Co. New York. 1970.
Beastly Bugs. Steve Parker. Raintree Steck-Vaughn. Austin, TX. 1994.
Beetles. Sylvia Johnson. Lerner Publications. Minneapolis. 1982.
The Big Bug Book. Margery Facklam. Little, Brown and Co. Boston.
    1994.
Butterflies (Animal Information). Elizabeth Kaufman. Price Stern
    Sloan. Los Angeles. 1988.
Butterflies (Life Story). Michael Chinery. Troll Associates. Mahwah,
    NJ. 1990.
Butterflies and Moths (Eyewitness Explorers). Steve Parker. Dorling
    Kindersley. New York. 1993.
Butterfly. Moira Butterfield. Simon & Schuster. New York. 1992.
Butterfly Express. Jane Belk Moncure. American Education Publishing.
    Columbus, OH. 1993.
Butterfly (See How They Grow). Mary Ling. Dorling Kindersley. New
    York. 1992.
Chirping Insects. Sylvia Johnson. Lerner Publications. Minneapolis.
    1986.
Cockroaches. Mona Kerby. Franklin Watts. New York. 1989.
Creepy Crawlies. Insects and Other Tiny Animals. Sue Jacquemier. EDC
    Publ. Oklahoma City. 1982.
Discover Butterflies. Gary A. Dunn. Publications International.
    Lincolnwood, IL. 1992.
Dragonflies. Cynthia Overbeck. Lerner Publications. Minneapolis, MN.
    1982.
Dragonfly. Emery and Durga Bernhard. Holiday House. New York. 1993.
Dragonfly. Barrie Watts. Silver Burdett Press. Englewood Cliffs, NJ.
    1988.
Extinct Insects and Those in Danger of Extinction. Philip Steele.
    Franklin Watts. New York. 1991.

Extremely Weird Insects. Sarah Lovett. John Muir Publications. Santa Fe, NM. 1992.

Fireflies. Sylvia Johnson. Lerner Publications. Minneapolis, MN. 1986.

Gnat. Andrienne Soutter-Perrot. American Education Publishing. 1993.

Good Bugs and Bad Bugs in Your Garden: Backyard Ecology. Dorothy Hogner. Harper and Row. New York. 1974.

Grass and Grasshoppers. Rose Wyler. Julian Messner. Englewood Cliffs, NJ. 1990.

Grasshoppers. Jane Dallinger. Lerner Publications. Minneapolis. 1981.

I Wonder Where Butterflies Go in Winter? Molly Marr. Western Publishing. Racine, WI. 1992.

Incredible Mini-beasts. Christopher Maynard. Covent Garden Books. New York. 1994.

Insects (Eyewitness Explorers). Steve Parker. Dorling Kindersley. New York. 1992.

Insects in the Garden. D.M. Souza. Carolrhoda Books. Minneapolis. 1991.

Insects Do the Strangest Things. Leonora and Arthur Hornblow. Random House. New York. 1990.

Insect Metamorphosis. Ron and Nancy Goor. Atheneum. New York. 1990.

Insects. (A New True Book). Illa Podendorf. Childrens Press. Chicago. 1981.

Insects. Rena Kirkpatrick. Raintree Steck-Vaughn. Austin, TX. 1991.

Insects. (Through the Microscope). John Stidworthy. Gloucester Press. New York. 1989.

Insects and Spiders. Lorus & Marjory Milne. Doubleday. New York. 1992.

It's a Good Thing There Are Insects. Allan Fowler. Childrens Press. Chicago. 1990.

Ladybug. Emery and Durga Bernhard. Holiday House. New York. 1992.

Ladybugs. Sylvia Johnson. Lerner Publications. Minneapolis. 1983.

Life of the Butterfly. H. & A. Fischer-Nagel. Carolrhoda Books. Minneapolis. 1987.

Life of the Honeybee. H. & A. Fischer-Nagel. Carolrhoda Books. Minneapolis. 1986.

Life of the Ladybug. H. & A. Fischer-Nagel. Carolrhoda Books. Minneapolis. 1986.

Marvels and Mysteries of Insect Life. Jennifer Owen. EDC Publ. Oklahoma City. 1984.

Michael Berenstain's Butterfly Book. Michael Berenstain. Western Publishing. Racine, WI. 1992.

Monarch Butterfly. Gail Gibbons. Holiday House. New York. 1989.

Monarchs. Kathryn Lasky. Harcourt Brace and Co. New York. 1993.

Pond Life. Rena Kirkpatrick. Raintree Steck-Vaughn. Austin, TX. 1991.

Puddles and Ponds. Rose Wyler. Julian Messner. Englewood Cliffs, NJ. 1990.

A Shimmer of Butterflies. Joni Hunt. Blake Publishing. San Luis Obispo. 1992.

Wasps. Sylvia Johnson. Lerner Publications. Minneapolis. 1984.

Water Insects. Sylvia Johnson. Lerner Publ. Co. Minneapolis. 1989.

What's Inside Insects? S. Whillock and J. Norsworthy. Dorling Kindersley. New York. 1992.

Where Butterflies Grow. Joanne Ryder. E.P. Dutton. New York. 1989.

The Young Scientist Investigates Pond Life. Terry Jennings. Childrens Press. Chicago. 1985.

The Young Scientist Investigates Small Garden Animals. Terry Jennings. Childrens Press. Chicago. 1982.

INSECT STUDY LESSON PLANS

The following section is designed to assist you in planning an insect study unit. Collectively, the key points listed in these lessons form a conceptual framework for entomology youth education and constitute a core curriculum for the study of insects. They are arranged in a logical order, starting with the basic facts about insects, followed by more complex concepts that integrate the basic topics, and finally culminating with insect interactions with other plants and animals, including humans. It is not my intention to provide complete, step-by-step instructions for each and every project and activity suggested in this manual. Many of the activity suggestions are exactly that ... suggestions! Enough basic information is given so that you can get started with planning and running each activity, but the final outcome of these activities will be determined by your own ingenuity and inventiveness. Feel free to experiment with these suggestions and adapt them to your students needs and skills.

I have provided activity appropriateness ratings so that you will have some idea of level of difficulty for each activity. Keep in mind that these are merely guidelines - the actual appropriateness will vary considerably according to the abilities of the children and yourself. The appropriateness categories are: P = pre-school, E = elementary, and I = intermediate (upper elementary and middle school). This information is also accompanied by information on the subject areas covered by the activity (e.g., art, human development, language arts, math, science, or social studies) and skills (analysis, application, classification, communication, comparing similarities and differences, creativity, computation, cooperation, decision-making, description, drawing, estimating, evaluation, experimentation, hypothesizing, identification, inference, interpretation, interview, invention, listening, listing, mapping, matching, measuring, motor skills, observation, prediction, problem-solving, public speaking, recognition, reporting, research, sequencing, small group work, synthesis, visualization, vocabulary and writing).

Furthermore, you may want to familiarize yourself with the information and ideas given in the many references cited below and elsewhere in this manual. This will further assist you in choosing the topics and activities you wish to cover in your insect study unit.

Many inexpensive resources available from the Young Entomologists' Society and other sources can be used to bring real excitement to your lessons (contact Y.E.S. for a free catalog).

References: Teaching and Activity Books for Teachers*

1001 Questions Answered About Insects. Alexander and Elie Klots. Dover Publications. New York. 1961.
Adventures with a Hand Lens. Richard Headstrom. Dover. New York. 1976.
Adventures with Freshwater Animals. Richard Headstrom. Dover Publ. Co. New York. 1964.

* Many of these books are available through the Y.E.S. "Buggy Bookstore". For a current catalog, or to check on availability, contact the Young Entomologists' Society, Inc., 1915 Peggy Place, Lansing, MI 48910-2553, phone (517) 887-0499

Adventures with Insects. Richard Headstrom. Dover Publ. New York. 1982.

Animal Activities: Insects. Jan Ormesher. Judy/Instructo. Minneapolis MN. 1987.

Ants and More Ants. Bev McKay. Incentive Publications. Nashville, TN. 1992.

Bats, Butterflies and Bugs. A Book of Action Toys. S. Adams Sullivan. Little, Brown and Co. Boston. 1991.

A Beginner's Guide to Observing and Collecting Insects. Gary A. Dunn. Young Entomologists' Society. Lansing, MI. 1994.

Boogie Woogie Bugs Activity Book. Don Cooper. Random House. New York. 1989. (includes cassette tape with songs)

Buggy Books. A Guide to Juvenile and Popular Books on Insects and their Relatives. Gary A. Dunn. Young Entomologists' Society. Lansing, MI. 1990.

BugPlay. Activities with Insects for Young Children. Marlene Hapai and Leon Burton. Addison-Wesley. Reading, MA. 1990.

Bugs and Other Insects. Using Nonfiction to Promote Literacy Across the Curriculum. Doris Roettger. Fearon Teacher Aids. Carthage, IL. 1991.

Bugs, Beetles and Butterflies (Experiences for Literacy) - Teachers Guide. Roach Van Allen, Michael Sampson and William Teale. DLM Teaching Resources. Allen, TX. 1989.

Bugs and Other Insects.. Doris Roettger. Fearon, Minneapolis. 1991.

Bugs, Beetles and Butterflies (Experiences for Literacy) - Teachers Guide. Roach Van Allen, Michael Sampson and William Teale. DLM Teaching Resources. Allen, TX. 1989.

Bugs, Bugs, Bugs. Better Homes and Gardens. Des Moines. 1989.

BugWise. Pamela Hickman. Addison-Wesley. Reading, MA. 1990.

The Butterfly Curriculum (K-2). Anonymous. Insect Lore Products. Shafter, CA. 19??.

The Butterfly Curriculum (3-6). Anonymous. Insect Lore Products. Shafter, CA. 19??.

The Butterfly Curriculum (JHS). Anonymous. Insect Lore Products. Shafter, CA. 19??.

The Butterfly Curriculum (HS). Anonymous. Insect Lore Products. Shafter, CA. 19??.

Buzzing a Hive. (Teachers Guide). Jean Echols. Univ. of California. Berkeley, CA. 1987.

Caring for Insect Livestock: An Insect Rearing Manual. Gary A. Dunn. Young Entomologists' Society. Lansing, MI. 1993.

Creepy Crawlies (Thematic Unit). Mary Ellen Sterling. Teacher Created Materials. Huntington Beach, CA. 1990.

Creepy Crawlies and the Scientific Method. Sally Stenhouse Kneidel. Fulcrum Publishing. Golden, CO. 1993

Critters. Anonymous. AIMS Education Foundation, Fresno. 1992.

Discover Butterflies! LuAnn Craighton. Isa Callaway Foundation. Pine Mountain, GA. 1991

Discovering Ants and Spiders. Peter and Connie Roop. Perfection Learning Corp. Logan, IA. 1992.

Draw 50 Creepy Crawlies. Lee J. Ames. Doubleday. New York. 1991.

Entertaining with Insects. Or, The Original Guide to Insect Cookery. Ronald Taylor. Woodbridge Press. Santa Barbara, CA. 1976

Entomology Projects for Elementary and Secondary Schools. John A. Wilcox. NY State Museum and Science Service. Albany, NY. 1972.

Entomology: Real Kids, Real Science. Ellen Doris. Thames and Hudson. New York. 1993.

A Guide to Observing Insect Lives. Donald Stokes. Little, Brown and Co. Boston. 1983.

Handbook for Butterfly Watchers. Robert Michael Pyle. Houghton
    Mifflin. Boston. 1992.
Hide a Butterfly Teacher's Guide). Jean Echols. University of
    California. Berkeley, CA. 1986.
Incredible Insects. (NatureScope). Judy Braus. National Wildlife
    Federation. Vienna, VA. 1988.
Incredible Insects Discovery Pac (NatureScope). Judy Braus. National
    Wildlife Federation. Vienna, VA. 1988.
The Insect Almanac. Monica Russo. Sterling Publ. Co. New York. 1991.
The Insect Appreciation Digest. F. Tom Turpin. Entomological
    Foundation. Lanham, MD. 1992.
Insect Biology. 49 Science Fair Projects. H. Steven Dashefsky. TAB
    Books. Blue Ridge Summit, PA. 1992.
The Insect Identification Guide. Gary A. Dunn. Young Entomologists'
    Society. Lansing, MI. 1994
Insects. (Full Options Science Systems.) Lawrence Hall of Science,
    Univ. of California. Berkeley. 1993.
Insects Did It First. Roger Akre, George Paulson, and Paul Catts. Ye
    Galleon Press. Fairfield, WA. 1992.
Insect Study Sourcebook. Gary A. Dunn. Young Entomologists' Society.
    Lansing, MI. 1992.
Investigating Insects Through Literature. Kathleen Myers. Perfection
    Learning Corp. Logan, IA. 1994.
Investigating Intriguing Insects. Stella Pallas. Foxtail Press. La
    Habra, CA. 1986.
Investigating Nature Through Outdoor Projects. Vinson Brown. Stackpole
    Books. Harrisburg, PA. 1983.
Insects in the Classroom. John Borden and Brian Herrin. British
    Columbia Teachers' Federation. Vancouver, BC. 1972.
Jellyfish to Insects: Projects with Science. William Hemsley.
    Gloucester Press. New York. 1991.
Ladybugs (Teacher's Guide). Jean C. Echols. Lawrence Hall of Science,
    Univ. of California. Berkeley, CA. 1993.
The Life Cycle of Butterflies (Teacher's Guide). Seliesa Pembleton and
    Patricia McGlashen. Carolina Biol. Supply Co. Burlington, NC. 1992.
Looking at Insects. David Suzuki. John Wiley and Sons. New York.
    1991.
Magical Migrating Monarchs. Judith and Lisa Levicoff. Jenkintown, PA.
    1993.
Monkeyshines Goes Buggy. The Study of Entomology. Phyllis Goldman.
    Monkeyshines Magazine. Greensboro, NC. 1992.
Naturewatch. Exploring Nature with Your Children. Adrienne Katz.
    Addison-Wesley Publishing. Reading, MA. 1986.
Organizing Bug Days and Insect Fairs. Gary A. Dunn. Young
    Entomologists' Society. Lansing, MI 1994.
The Practical Entomologist. Rick Imes. Simon & Schuster. New York.
    1992.
Should Bugs Bug You? (Teacher Edition). Beau Fly Jones. Zaner-Blosser.
    Columbus, OH. 1990.
Studying Insects. Edward Ortleb and Richard Cadice. Milliken Publ. St
    Louis, MO. 1986. (beautiful color overhead transparencies)
Using Live Insects in Elementary Classroom for Early Lessons in Life.
    Anonymous. Center for Insect Science Education Outreach, University
    of Arizona. Tucson, AZ. 1993.
Young Scientist Investigates Pond Life. Terry Jennings. Childrens
    Press. Chicago, IL. 1985.
Young Scientist Investigates Small Garden Animals. Terry Jennings.
    Childrens Press. Chicago, IL. 1982.

Lesson 1: INSECT AWARENESS AND APPRECIATION

In your first lesson you will "set the stage" for the entire insect study unit. It's important to create the right atmosphere and to share some of the things that the students will be learning as part of the unit. You may also want to evaluate the children's knowledge and attitude about insects to help in final planning for your other lessons.

Key Points

1. Young people are usually fascinated by insects and insect study is a way for them to learn more about insect types, life cycles, behaviors, habitats, and relationships with humans.

2. Insects are very important in our world and this often gets overlooked. There are more insects in the world than all other animals combined. About 90% of all animals are insects (there are at least 10 million different species). Insects are also the most abundant animals in terms of the number of individuals of each of these ten million species.

3. Some insect species have inhabited the planet for at least 300 million years. We know this because of the fossil record that insects have left behind. Some insects have changed very little since the dawn of time, other have changed greatly, and some have become extinct.

Activity Ideas

The Forgotten Animals Quiz. Insects are some of the most amazing animals that inhabit our world, yet most of us rarely give them credit for their incredible abilities. The "Forgotten Animal Quiz" will help children "tune in" to the incredible world of insects and help open their eyes and minds to learning about insects.

Have the children number a piece of paper down the left hand side from 1 to 25. Tell them that you will be reading a series of short statements and that they should write down the name of an ANIMAL that fits the description.

NAME AN ANIMAL THAT ....

```
 (1) .... raids the garbage
 (2) .... is cold blooded
 (3) .... hides from other animals by using camouflage
 (4) .... changes shape as it grows
 (5) .... is poisonous and covered with scales
 (6) .... lives in the ground
 (7) .... is capable of flying
 (8) .... attacks and devours (eats) other animals
 (9) .... migrates long distances
(10) .... gathers and stores food
(11) .... sings to attract a mate
(12) .... hibernates as an adult
(13) .... eats wood
(14) .... lives longer than 40 years
(15) .... is striped
(16) .... lives on another animal
(17) .... spends part of its life cycle in the water
```

(18) .... drinks nectar from flowers
(19) .... lays eggs
(20) .... has big back legs and is a good hopper
(21) .... catches their prey with traps
(22) .... is active mostly at night
(23) .... is brightly colored
(24) .... is covered with hairs
(25) .... gives off a foul odor

After administering the quiz score them in the following manner: 1 point of each mammal named; 3 points for each bird/reptile/amphibian/fish; and 5 points for each arthropod (insects, spider, etc.). In this game* you get more points when you name insects for your answer!

A few of the possible arthropod (insect/spider) answers are: (1) fly/maggot, carrion beetle; (2) any insect or other arthropod!; (3) walkingstick, underwing moth, crab spider; (4) any insect or other arthropod!; (5) monarch butterfly; (6) ant, yellowjacket, white grub/beetle; (7) fly, bee, wasp, ant, moth, butterfly, beetle, bug, grasshopper, dragonfly, mayfly, caddisfly - in fact, most adult insects!; (8) praying mantis, ladybird beetle, aphidlion, wolf spider, tarantula, centipede; (9) monarch butterfly, painted lady butterfly, green darner dragonfly, leafhopper; (10) ant, honey bee; (11) cicada, cricket, katydid; (12) morningcloak butterfly, ladybird beetle; (13) termite, wood-boring beetle (not ants!); (14) queen termite; (15) bee, monarch (caterpillar), swallowtail (caterpillar), beetle; (16) louse, flea, tick; (17) dragonfly, damselfly, mosquito, stonefly, mayfly, caddisfly; (18) butterfly, moth, bee, fly; (19) any insect; (20) grasshopper, cricket, leafhopper, flea, flea beetle; (21) antlion, spider; (22) moth, most beetles; (23) many butterflies and beetles; (24) mosquito, caddisfly, many caterpillars; (25) stink bug, bombardier beetle, black swallowtail caterpillar.

(* - quiz concept by Diane Valen, Dahlem Environmental Education Center, Jackson, MI) [Levels: E/I; Subjects: science/language arts; Skills: decision-making/listening/listing]

What Do We Know About Insects? Talk with the children about the topic of insects, but let them do most of the talking so you can find out what they already know about insects. After a brief introduction to your unit on insects, have the children list five reasons why they might be interested in studying insects. Have them share their lists. Write down the information as it is given, for example:

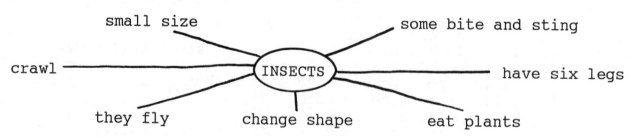

Help the children organize (classify) the information and list it under appropriate headings, for example:

Physical Features	Movement	Behavior	Food
small size	crawl	bite/sting	eat leaves
six legs	fly	change shape	

Post the chart in an accessible and visible location. As additional information is gathered during the course of the unit, periodically add it to the chart. Where necessary, create additional headings and delete/correct misinformation. [Levels: P/E/I; Subjects: science/language arts; Skills: charting/classifying/communicating/listing]

Insect Name Calling. Ask the children to name any five insects they can think of. If possible, write the names on a blackboard, overhead projector, or large pad of paper so that everybody can see them. After the list is made (no more insects can be named by the children), go over it and make mention of any non-insects that may have been listed. The data (names) you collect can also be used to make a chart (of the insects most familiar to the class). You may want to repeat this exercise at the end of the unit, so save the list for comparison. [Levels: E/I; Subjects: science/language arts; Skills: charting/ communication/listening/listing]

Insect Alphabet. This activity is similar to the preceding, and makes a great group charting activity. Prepare a large poster that features all the letters of the alphabet on the left side and lots of space on the right side. As an alternative you can also make 26 separate miniposters, each with a letter at the top of the page. The challenge is for the children to think of insect names for the appropriate letters of the alphabet (you may have to act as "recorder", depending on their age). Which letter do you think will have the longest list? There's only one way to find out. You might want to prepare a graph of the data collected to show the results in a more visual manner. [Levels: P/E/I; Subjects: language arts; Skills: listing/charting and graphing]

Pass Me the Grasshopper! This insect naming activity will probably have greater appeal to younger children. The only item you will need for this activity is an insect bean bag. You can make one from a fabric with pre-printed designs of insects, or you can use an insect bean bag (available from a local toy store or the Young Entomologists' Society). Have the children form a circle and then instruct them on how to play the game. They will pass the bean bag around the circle to the left (or right if you prefer); the recipient of the bean bag gets to name an insect. If they can't think of an insect, or they name one that has already been mentioned, they should toss the bean bag across the circle. Play until the group runs out of names, or gets tired. [Levels: P/E; Subjects: science/human development; Skills: communication/cooperation/motor skills]

Insect Words From A to Z. If your curriculum includes a letter of the day/week theme, or if you like to introduce new vocabulary words within a theme, then you should consider using an alphabetic word chart (see the glossary at the end of this book for definitions and pronunciations for a wide variety of entomological words). Some of the words may at first appear too advanced, but many educators believe that children like to learn long words with interesting sounds, so don't be afraid to try these out. [Levels: P/E; Subjects: science/language arts; Skills: classification/listening/ listing/vocabulary]

Insect Word Bank. During the course of your investigation of insects you and the children will encounter many new words and unfamiliar terms. While working on your insect studies, develop a word list (word bank) together. Each day you will want to review new words or terms that the group has encountered and discuss their meaning (see the glossary in the back of this book). Organize the words in alphabetical (ABC) order. You can use large index cards to record each new word (along with its meaning, and a drawing if necessary); post them where the children can refer to them as needed. For older children you may want to organize them in a card catalog. [Levels: P/E/I; Subjects: science/language arts; Skills: classification/listing/writing]

Buggy Expressions and Words. Have each child create a list of everyday expressions and words that are entomological figures of speech. For example, "Bah! Humbug!", "getting the bugs worked out", "fly in the ointment", "shutter-bug", "fly ball", "beeline", etc. Have the children share their lists and make a combined list for the group on a chart, chalkboard, or overhead. I think the group will be surprised by the number of ways in which insect words have found their way into our language! [Levels: E/I; Subjects: science/language arts; Skills: listing/vocabulary/writing]

Hey, Have You Heard This One? Just for the fun of it, try some tongue twisters, riddles, or jokes about insects (see references, page 35). Don't forget to let the children participate in the reading where appropriate. Younger children might enjoy making bug masks to wear as they participate in the jokes or riddles. [Levels: P/E/I; Subject: language arts; Skills: listening/public speaking/reading]

Bug Poetry Reading. There are several good books filled with poems about insects (see booklist on page 35). Share some of these poems with the children by reading them out loud. If you want to involve the children, I suggest using "Joyful Noise: Poems for Two Voices" by Paul Fleichman. These poems, done in duet, are really great, and older children should have no problem assisting you with a performance of Fleichman's poems. Some of the poems can even be acted out by the children. Younger children might enjoy making bug masks to wear as they participate in the poetry reading. [Levels: P/E/I; Subjects: language arts/art; Skills: listening/public speaking/reading/visualization]

Word Chains. A word chain is a string of words that starts with the same letter and communicates some information on a chosen subject. For example: Scary spiders spin silken snares to snatch six-legged specimens as snacks. As you can see it was necessary to use a few short "connecting" words so that the statement reads more sensibly. Have the children pick a favorite insect, and then let them get creative! [Levels: E/I; Subjects: science/language arts; Skills: communication/description/vocabulary]

Give Me a Pound of Bugs, Please. Insects are the most numerous type of animals on our planet. It has been estimated that the biomass (combined weight) of just the ants would exceed the biomass of all other living things put together. That's a lot of ants! Have the children calculate how many insects it would take to make a pound (or other unit of measure) for each of several different species. For example, an African goliath beetle weighs 4 ounces (1/4 pound); a Madagascar hissing cockroach weighs 1/4 ounce; and an aphid weighs less than 1/1000 of an ounce. Have each student calculate how many goliath beetles, Madagascar hissing roaches, and aphids it would take to equal their own weight. As an extension of this activity, collect a small sample of common insects from your area and weigh them (you will find that most insects will have to be weighed as a group, using division to find the weight for an individual). Calculate the biomass for one thousand individuals, ten thousand individuals, one hundred thousand individuals, and a million individuals. [Levels: E/I; Subjects: science/math; Skills: computation]

It's a Good Thing There Are Insects. Discuss what the world would be like without insects as pollinators, food for animals, and recyclers (decomposers). What changes would take place if all insects suddenly died tomorrow? What would life be like for people and other animals? (Hint: These makes a great topic for a brief paragraph or essay for older children.) You might also have the children ponder what the world would be like without human beings! Would the world come to a stop? [Levels: E/I; Subjects: science/language arts; Skills: communication/critical thinking/hypothesizing/ predicting/writing]

Fact or Fiction? Insects do some truly amazing things, but can the children distinguish fact from fiction? Try using some of the questions from the following "Insect Quiz" to evaluate their knowledge about insects. [Levels: E/I; Subject: science; Skills: critical thinking/ listening/synthesis]

Insects stop growing when they become adults. <u>True</u> or False.
There are more species of insects than all other animal species combined. <u>True</u> or False.
Fireflies glow because of electricity. True or <u>False</u>.
The vampire moth of Australia sucks blood. <u>True</u> or False.
The bombardier beetle shoots a boiling-hot liquid at its enemies. <u>True</u> or False.
You can't die from a single bee sting. True or <u>False</u>.
A fairyfly is so small it can fly through the eye of a needle. <u>True</u> or False.
Some aquatic insects live in natural hot springs with near-boiling water. <u>True</u> or False.
Honey bees must make between 50 and 100 round trips to collect enough nectar to make a pound of honey. <u>True</u> or False.
Only female mosquitoes bite and suck blood. <u>True</u> or False.
Queen bees can't sting. True or <u>False</u>.
There are no male (boy) ladybugs. True or <u>False</u>.
The only fully domesticated insect is the Chinese silkworm <u>True</u> or False.
Bee venom has been used to treat arthritis. <u>True</u> or False.
Insects invented paper. <u>True</u> or False.
Mosquitoes can sting. True or <u>False</u>.
Insects have traveled in space. <u>True</u> or False.
Dragonflies can sting. True or <u>False</u>.
A honey bee can sting more than once. True or <u>False</u>.
The lightningbug is really a beetle. <u>True</u> or False.
There are more species of beetles than all other animal species combined. <u>True</u> or False.
You can tell the age of a ladybug by counting its spots. True or <u>False</u>.
Worker ants are males (boys). True or <u>False</u>.
Most insects have yellow, not red, blood. <u>True</u> or False.
Bees taste with their feet. <u>True</u> or False.
Some insects live under the snow. <u>True</u> or False.
The flea is the smallest insect. True or <u>False</u>.
The world's longest insect is a walkingstick from Malaysia that is 13" long. <u>True</u> or False.
The cockroach is a living fossil, and unlike most other insects was around during the days of the dinosaurs. <u>True</u> or False.
Insects only live for one year or less. True or <u>False</u>.
The short circuit beetle gnaws holes in lead-sheathed telephone cables causing electrical short circuits. <u>True</u> or False.

Insects were the first flying animals. <u>True</u> or False.
Insects breath with tiny little lungs. True or <u>False</u>.
A grasshopper can leap about 20 times the length of its body. <u>True</u> or
    False.
Army ants get their name because of their green color. True or <u>False</u>.
Plant lice can infest people too. True or <u>False</u>.
Insects stop growing when they become adults. <u>True</u> or False.

If I Were an Insect. Have the children write or tell a story about what it would be like to be an insect (keeping in mind that grass blades would be like trees, pebbles like boulders, and dogs like huge monsters, just like in the movie "Honey I Shrunk the Kids"). What would it be like to a member of an ant colony or wasp nest? How would it feel to fly long distances? How can you escape from danger? What's it like to be a flea on the back of a dog? Check out some of the great books listed below. [Levels: E/I; Subject: language arts; Skills: communication/public speaking/writing]

Bring Out the Banners! To increase awareness and appreciation for insects, have the children work in small groups to create a series of colorful banners that feature members of the insect world. These banners can be made from felt (or other cloth not prone to unraveling) or paper. The banners can be decorated with crayons, markers, paints, glitter, or rubber stamps and ink. Additional items such as straws, beads, chenilles, doll eyes, and pom-poms can be used to make the banners 3-D. [Levels: P/E/I/; Subjects: science/art; Skills: cooperation/drawing/measuring/motor skills/small group work]

References

Joyful Noise: Poems for Two Voices. Paul Fleischman. Harper and Row,
    New York. 1988.
If I Were An Ant. Amy Moses. Childrens Press. Chicago. 1992.
If You Were An Ant. S.J. Calder. Silver Press. Englewood Cliffs, NJ.
    1989.
Insects Did it First. Roger Akre, Gregory Paulson and Paul Catts. Ye
    Galleon Press. Fairfield, WA. 1992.
Insects Do the Strangest Things. Leonora and Arthur Hornblow. Random
    House. New York. 1990.
It's a Good Thing There Are Insects. Allan Fowler. Childrens Press.
    Chicago, IL.
Mysteries and Marvels of the Insect World. Jennifer Owen. EDC
    Publishing. Oklahoma City, OK. 1984.
Step by Step. Diane Wolkstein. Morrow Junior Books. New York. 1994.

FAVORITE INSECT SURVEY

Use the following chart to record a person's favorite insect from among the choices illustrated below. Asking different groups (one class vs. another, children vs. adults) will probably give different results.

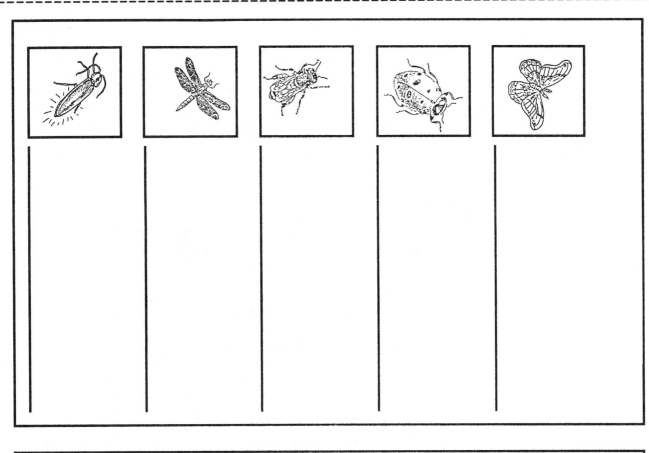

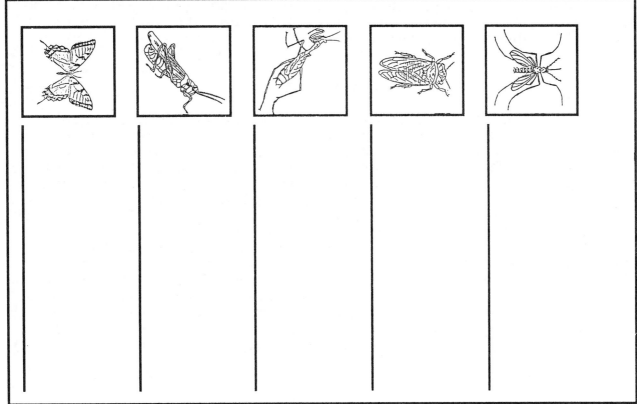

Lesson 2: WHAT IS AN INSECT?

The answer to this question is the basis for all of the other insect studies you will undertake as a part of your insect unit. After all, it's very important to know which animals are insects and which ones are not.

Key Points

1. Insects belong to the phylum ARTHROPODA. Arthropods are small animals with an external skeleton (exoskeleton). Because arthropods have their bones on the outside, their bodies must be segmented and jointed to allow movement. It's important to be able to distinguish insects from the other arthropod groups, such as ticks, spiders, scorpions, centipedes, millipedes, and crustaceans. The arthropods can be distinguished by the number of body sections, number of legs, and the presence or absence of antennae and/or wings.

ARTHROPOD GROUP	BODY PARTS	LEGS	EYES	ANTENNAE?	WINGS?
Insects	3	6	compound & simple	1 pair	0-2 pair
Spiders, Ticks and Mites	2	8	simple	none	none
Centipedes	2	30-60	simple	1 pair	none
Millipedes	2	>60	compound	1 pair	none
Crustaceans	2	14-22	simple	1-2 pair	none

2. Insects belong to the class INSECTA (sometimes known as HEXAPODA, meaning six feet - a reference to the fact that all insects have six legs). Insects are arthropods with an exoskeleton (like all arthropods), three body parts, six legs, one pair of antennae, two sets of eyes (simple and compound), and wings (usually).

Activity Ideas

Insects and Spiders and Arthropods. Ask the children to identify the characteristics that help distinguish insects from other animals (exoskeleton, three body parts, six legs, compound eyes, antennae, and wings). Now, which of these characteristics are useful in separating insects from the other arthropod groups such as spiders, centipedes, millipedes, and crustaceans? Review your list and point out how they all have an exoskeleton, so this characteristic is only useful in separating arthropods from other animal groups. (Note: You may want to create a fill-in-the-blank chart, similar to the one shown above, so that the children can supply the missing information and achieve a better understanding of how insects differ from the other non-insect arthropods. For younger children it's a good idea to make the chart extra large so that there will also be room for a picture of a representative from each group.) Or, use the Venn diagram on page 54. [Levels: E/I; Subject: science; Skills: classification/comparing similarities and differences/ identification]

Arthropod Family Tree. Construct an "arthropod family tree" showing how various arthropods are related to one another. This can be done as a large poster, bulletin board, or mobile. If you have the space and really want to get fancy, you can also use a real tree branch (set upright in a plaster or pebble-filled bucket) to hang your pictures on. In any case try to arrange the "branches" so that the most closely related members of the phylum Arthropoda are near each other (see figure on page 55). Choose two main branches to represent the subphyla Chelicerata (arthropods with fang-like mouthparts) and the subphyla Mandibulata (arthropods with mandibles or jaws). For example, spiders, ticks, mites, and scorpions would be grouped near each other, while the millipedes, centipedes, crustaceans, and insects would be grouped separately. Then select smaller branches for each class and order (again see the figure on page 55). Make sure you leave enough room on each branch to place pictures of representative "family" members. [Levels: P/E/I; Subject: science; Skills: classification/comparing similarities and differences/visualization]

The Bug Swap Game. To play this game you will need a small collection of insect and arthropod pictures (simple drawings or sketches will do), or a collection of rubber "bugs". You will need at least two pictures or rubber "bugs" for as many arthropod groups as possible (e.g., insects, spiders, ticks, mites, scorpions, daddy-long-legs, centipedes, millipedes, crustaceans, and horseshoe crabs). You will need enough pictures or rubber "bugs" so that each child has one (or more) picture or rubber bug. Ask the children to sit on the floor in a circle. As you call out the name of an arthropod group, the children who have those pictures/rubber bugs should change places with one another. Then call out another arthropod group. Play until each child has had at least one turn. [Levels: P/E; Subject: science; Skills: classification/comparing similarities and differences/cooperation/motor skills/observation/recognition]

Whose Shadow is That? Rubber arthropod replicas (available from toy/novelty stores or the Young Entomologists' Society) can be placed on an overhead projector so as to project a large shadow of a "mystery bug" for the children to identify. In order to keep the identity of each "mystery bug" a secret it will be necessary to build a cardboard "privacy screen" around the front and sides of the projector. This activity will sharpen observation skills and allow the children to identify various arthropods by studying similarities and differences in the shape of the body, number of body sections, number of legs, and presence/absence of antennae and/or wings. [Levels: P/E/I; Subject: science; Skills: classification/comparing similarities and differences/cooperation/observation/recognition]

REFERENCES

Invertebrates. Lionel Bender. Gloucester Press, New York. 1988.
Invertebrate Zoology: Real Kids/Real Science. Ellen Dores. Thames and Hudson, New York. 1993.
Jellyfish to Insects: Projects with Science. William Hemsley. Gloucester Press, New York. 1991.
Spiders and their Kin. Herbert and Lorna Levi. Western Publishing. Racine, WI. 1990.

INSECT WORLD Activity Sheet
Insect and Spider Venn Diagram

Instructions: This activity sheet will help you explore the similarities and differences between insects and spiders. The Venn Diagram, consisting of two overlapping circles, will help you in sorting through your knowledge on these two arthropod groups (I think that was a hint!). The overlapping area in the center will contain information or statements that are true for both insects and spiders (similarities). The outer areas will contain information on insects (left) and spiders (right), the differences.

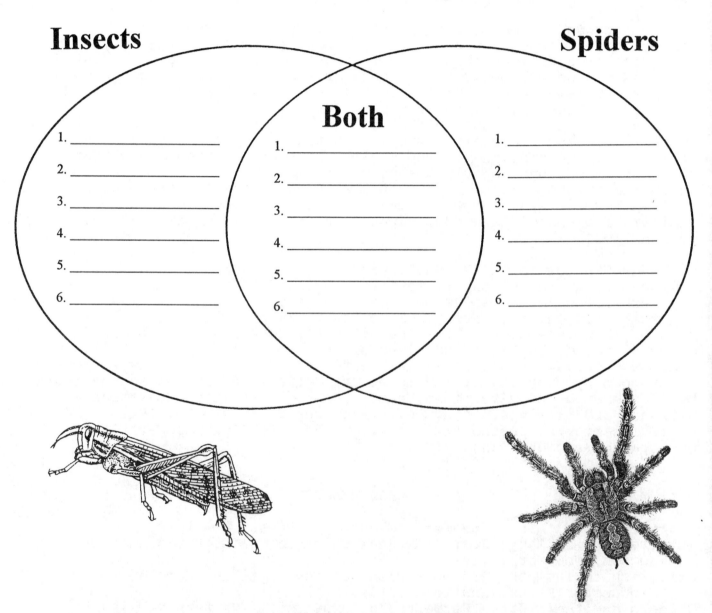

Insects

1. _____
2. _____
3. _____
4. _____
5. _____
6. _____

Both

1. _____
2. _____
3. _____
4. _____
5. _____
6. _____

Spiders

1. _____
2. _____
3. _____
4. _____
5. _____
6. _____

A reproducible resource from "PROJECT B.U.G.S." by Gary A. Dunn, published by the Young Entomologists' Society, Inc., 1915 Peggy Place, Lansing, MI 48910-2553, tel. (517) 887-0499.

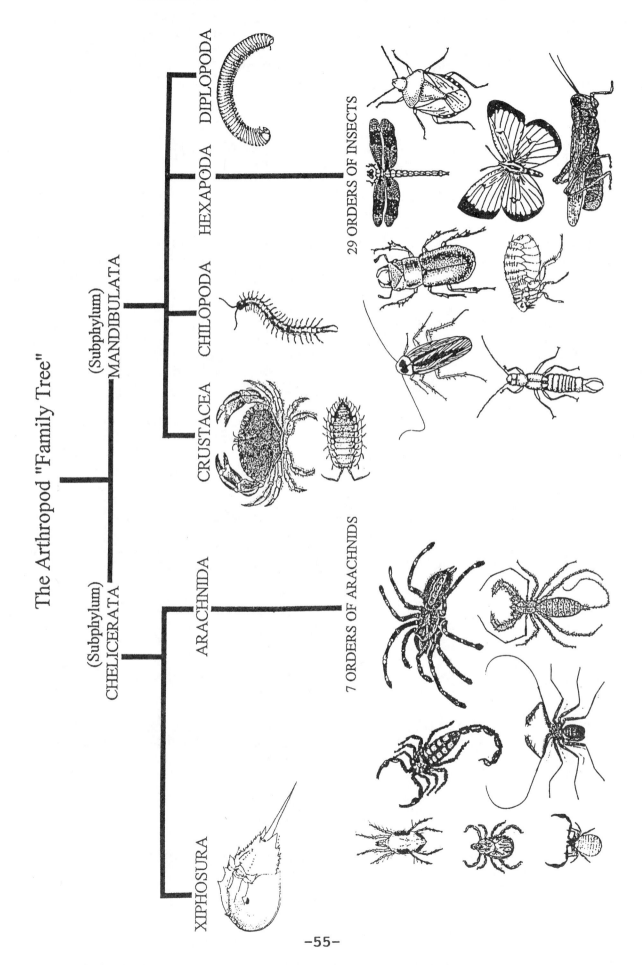

The Arthropod "Family Tree"

(Subphylum) MANDIBULATA

(Subphylum) CHELICERATA

DIPLOPODA

HEXAPODA

29 ORDERS OF INSECTS

CHILOPODA

CRUSTACEA

ARACHNIDA

7 ORDERS OF ARACHNIDS

XIPHOSURA

Lesson 3: INSECT BODIES

Now that the children can distinguish insects from other arthropods and animals, the next step is learning in greater detail how insect bodies are put together. This becomes particularly important for further discussions and investigations of insect identification and classification.

Key Points

1. Insects do not have bones inside their bodies. Instead they have a hard covering called an exoskeleton.

2. Insect bodies are composed of three major sections - the head, the thorax (where wings and legs are attached), and the abdomen.

3. Adult insects have six legs; some immature insects may lack legs or may have accessory legs (unjointed prolegs). Insect legs may be modified for jumping, holding and grasping, running, swimming, digging, or carrying pollen.

4. All insects have one pair of antennae on their heads. These are used to feel, smell, and in some insects, to hear, and taste food. Insect antennae may appear long and slender, short and bristle-like, bead-like, plume-like, elbowed, clubbed, or comb-like.

5. Adult insects almost always have wings, as a result many insects can fly. Most have two pairs of wings, but a few have one pair, and some lack wings altogether. The wings may be membranous, scaly, hairy, leathery, half-leathery and half-membranous, or armor-like.

6. Most insects have two sets of eyes, simple and compound. The compound eyes are large and composed of many separate ocular units. Many insects also have three simple eyes located on the head between the compound eyes. Some immature insects only have simple eyes.

7. Insects, depending on the species, can be as small as 1/100th of an inch or as large as 13" in length. The "average" insect is probably slightly less than 1/2 inch in length.

8. Most insects have tiny hairs on their bodies that are sensitive to movement, pressure, smell, and sound.

9. Insects have a simple circulatory system. The heart is open-ended and pumps blood through open body cavities; there are no closed vessels (arteries or veins). The blood is almost colorless.

Activity Ideas

Parts of An Insect. Large rubber insects (available from toy/novelty stores or the Young Entomologists' Society) can be used to show the body parts of an insect (or other groups of arthropods, too.). These "bugs" are easily handled by children of all ages and because of

-56-

their large size the various body parts can be easily seen without
magnification. First, see how many structures the children can identify.
As they point out different structures, you should provide some
information on their functions and modifications. If the children run out
of ideas, you can fill in with information on any structures that were not
mentioned. Most of the better rubber replicas are quite anatomically
correct, but you might have older children examine them for any incorrect
features. [Levels: P/E/I; Subject: science; Skills: communication/
comparing similarities and differences/observation/recognition]

Insect Body Part Song. Here is a song to help children remember the
basic parts of an insect's body. It is sung to the tune of "Head,
Shoulders, Knees, and Toes," and goes like this:

    Head, tho-rax, ab-do-men, ab-do-men
    Head, tho-rax, ab-do-men, ab-do-meh-eh-eh-en
    Six legs, some wings, and an ex-o-skel-eton
    Head, tho-rax, ab-do-men, ab-do-men

    Head, tho-rax, ab-do-men, ab-do-men
    Head, tho-rax, ab-do-men, ab-do-meh-eh-eh-en
    Big eyes, small size, and a pair of feel-ers, too
    Head, tho-rax, ab-do-men, ab-do-men

This song can also combined with movement. Have the children pretend
they are the insects, and as they sing they should point to their head,
thorax (point to chest) and abdomen (point to stomach), legs, wings (point
over their shoulder), exoskelton (arms up over head and make sweeping
motion down towards the feet), big eyes (hold hands up to eyes as if
looking through a pair of binoculars), small size (hold out thumb and
pointer finger to indicate small size), and feelers (put arms up over head
and wiggle pointer finger). [Levels: P/E; Subjects: science/arts/child
development; Skills: motor skills/singing/visualization]

Magnificent Model Hexapods.   Models are real objects that represent
something else. They can help children visualize and understand the
world, especially things that are too small to see, too big to see, too
dangerous to experiment with, no longer in existence, or not yet
invented. Have the children (individually or in small groups) make
"model" insects out of household materials such as construction paper,
paper plates, felt, pom-poms, cottonballs, styrofoam balls and shapes,
bottle caps, pipe cleaners, wire, dowels, buttons, beads, glitter, walnut
shells, macaroni, clothes pins, etc. Balloons and paper mache can also be
used to make insect models, as can modeling clay or claydough. Or, use
egg carton sections (three for an adult insect, six for a caterpillar).
Some really neat caddisfly cases can be made from toilet tissue or
papertowel tubes - cover one end and the outside with sticks, stones, or
leaves to give that authentic look. Now you can make a paper mache or
modeling clay caddisfly larva to place in the model caddisfly case. In a
similar manner a neat moth cocoon can be made by winding yarn around a
toilet paper tube or crumpled piece of paper.
As an extension of this activity, invite special guests (another
class, parents, principal, or local entomologist) to come and see the
children's creations, and give the children an opportunity to tell
something about their insect model. Or, have each child write a brief
report about their model, including how they put it together. Their
report should be detailed enough that somebody else could make a model
insect just like theirs. If time permits, you can also have them write a

make believe story about their model insect: where it lives, what it eats, noises it makes, etc. [Levels: P/E/I; Subjects: science/arts; Skills: creativity/motor skills/small group work/writing]

3-D Insect Puzzles. To better appreciate the structure and function of insect bodies, let the children experiment with any of the Insect Woodcraft Kits (available at local nature stores or through the Young Entomologists' Society) during free time. These kits are like a 3-dimensional puzzle of an insect body and they are as entertaining as they are educational. [Levels: E/I; Subjects: science/child development; Skills: decision-making/motor skills/visualization]

Insect Mug Shots. Use pictures of insects collected from books, magazines, calendars, information leaflets (USDA Extension Service - check with your county extension office or state landgrant university), or pesticide brochures to illustrate and discuss the following:
 - What types of mouthparts, legs, and wings can be seen?
 - Why do some insects have chewing mouthparts and other have piercing-sucking mouthparts? (Hint: what kind of food do they eat, solid or liquid.) Have the children find an example of different mouthpart types from the picture collection.
 - Why do they think insects have such a wide variety of leg and wing types? (Hint: these are usually modified to suit the insects special way of life.) Have the children find an example of different leg and wing types from the picture collection. [Level: E/I/J; Subject: science; Skills: comparing similarities and differences/inference/observation]

Name the Parts Diagrams. Make and/or use some simple diagrams of insects and have the children label the important body parts. Ready-to-use name the parts diagrams can be found on page 59 and 60. [Levels: E/I/J; Subject: science; Skills: recognition]

Build A Bug. Use layered overhead transparencies to "build a bug" and show the various body parts. You can make your own from name-the-parts diagrams, or you can buy ready-to-use sets available from Y.E.S. for a nominal price. [Levels: P/E/I; Subject: science; Skills: recognition]

Gossimer Wings. Set up a microscope (or other powerful magnifier) so that the children can look at a butterfly wing. Have them write a description of what they see, answering the following questions. What did the wing scales look like? What colors did they see? Could they tell if the colors were caused by pigments or reflections of light? Then have the children draw a picture of what they saw through the microscope. [Levels: E/I; Subjects: science/language arts/art; Skills: description/drawing/observation/prediction])

Anatomy Character Sorting. For this activity you will need a collection of insect pictures from magazines, books, calendars, or insect cards (available from the Young Entomologists' Society), and two boxes (or similar bins). Label a pair of bins with any of the following character pairs: walk/fly, wings/no wings, wings membranous/wings not membranous, aquatic/terrestrial, long antennae/short antennae, or chewing mouthparts/sucking mouthparts. Show each picture and have the children take turns telling which bin the picture should go in. If you relabel the bins (or have multiple bins made up) you can repeat the activity with each contrasting character set. [Levels: P/E/I; Subjects: science/human development; Skills: comparing similarities and differences/decision making]

INSECT WORLD Activity Sheet
Name-the-Parts Diagram

Instructions: Below is a diagram of a grasshopper, with many of its body parts identified only by numbers. There is also an alphabetic list of body parts. In the blank space to the left of each word write the number of the correct body part. Some numbers may be used more than once. (Answers are given below.)

__ antenna   __ coxa   __ hindwing   __ pronotum   __ tegmen
__ cercus   __ ear   __ labrum   __ simple eye   __ tergite
__ claw   __ femur   __ ocellus   __ spiracle   __ tibia
__ clypeus   __ forewing   __ ovipositor   __ sternite   __ trochanter
__ compound eye __ head   __ palp   __ tarsus   __ tympanum

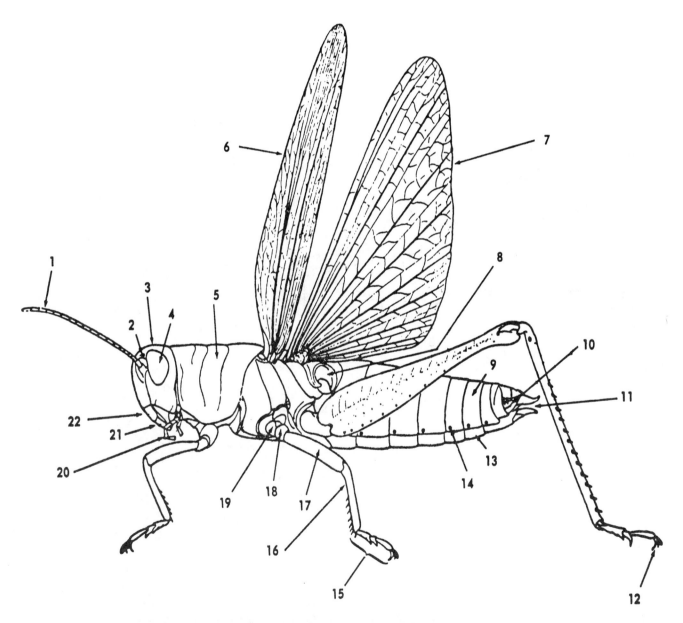

Answers: 1-antenna, 10-cercus, 12-claw, 22-clypeus, 4-compound eye, 19-coxa, 8-ear, 17-femur, 6-forewing, 3-head, 7-hindwing, 21-labrum, 2-ocellus, 11-ovipositor, 20-palp, 5-pronotum, 2-simple eye, 14-spiracle, 13-sternite, 15-tarsus, 6-tegmen, 9-tergite, 16-tibia, 18-trochanter, and 8-tympanum

A reproducible resource from "PROJECT B.U.G.S." by Gary A. Dunn, published by the Young Entomologists' Society, Inc., 1915 Peggy Place, Lansing, MI 48910-2553, tel. (517) 887-0499.

INSECT WORLD Activity Sheet
Name-the-Parts Diagram

Instructions: Below is a diagram of a beetle, with many of its body parts identified only by numbers. There is also an alphabetic list of body parts. In the blank space to the left of each word write the number of the correct body part. Some numbers may be used more than once. (Answers are given below.)

__ abdomen   __ elytron   __ hindwing   __ spiracle
__ antenna   __ femur   __ mandible   __ tarsus
__ claws   __ forewing   __ palps   __ tibia
__ compound eye   __ head   __ pronotum   __ vein

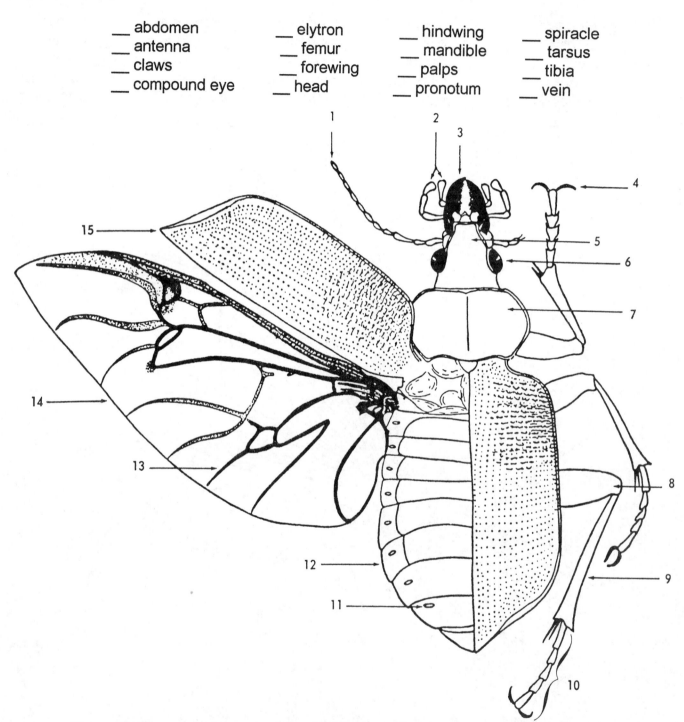

Answers: 12-abdomen, 1-antenna, 4-claws, 6-compound eye, 15-elytron, 8-femur, 15-forewing, 5-head, 14-hindwing, 3-mandible, 2-palps, 7-pronotum, 11-spiracle, 10-tarsus, 9-tibia, and 13-vein.

A reproducible resource from "PROJECT B.U.G.S." by Gary A. Dunn, published by the Young Entomologists' Society, Inc., 1915 Peggy Place, Lansing, MI 48910-2553, tel. (517) 887-0499.

Bug "Body Swap" Game. To play this game you will need a small collection of insect pictures or simple drawings of various insect body parts. There should be at least two pictures for each type of body part (chewing mouthpart & siphoning mouthpart, elbowed antenna & thread-like antenna, walking leg & swimming leg, membranous wing & scaly wing, etc.). You will need enough pictures so that each child has two pictures. Ask the children to sit on the floor in a circle. As you call out the name of a body part, the children who have those pictures should change places with one another. Then call out another body part. Play until each child has had at least one turn. [Levels: E/I; Subjects: science/human development; Skills: matching/observation]

Micro-monsters! Place some tiny insects (booklice, silverfish, springtails, thrips, aphids, or small beetles) in a petri dish under a microscope. Detailed information on how to collect these insects can be found in "A Beginner's Guide to Observing and Collecting Insects" by Gary A. Dunn (Young Entomologists' Society. 1994.) If the insects are overly active, chill them for a few minutes in a refrigerator or on some ice to slow them down. Give the students a chance to look at them. Describe how the smallest insects (fairyflies and feather-winged beetles) are so small that they can fly through the eye of a needle. What are the advantages of being small? (Greater utilization of habitat and food, ease of hiding, etc.) [Levels: P/E/I; Subject: science; Skills: observation]

Weird Insects. Have the children combine the names of two (or more) insects into a new name, for example dragonfly + flea = a dragonflea, or bumblebee + bed bug = a bumblebug. Now have them write a brief description (and or drawing) of the imaginary insect along with information on its habitat and food preferences. [Levels: P/E/I; Subjects: science/arts; Skills: creativity/description/writing]

Insect Olympics. For their size, insects are incredible strong creatures (due to an external skeleton and an internal musculature). The object of this activity is to help children compare their strength to that of various insects by removing the size differential. Each child will need to know their height (rounded to the nearest foot) and weight (rounded to the nearest pound). Have the children make the following calculations:

A grasshopper can jump 20X the length of its body.
If I were a grasshopper, I could jump ____ feet (my height x 20)

A male cicada can he heard as far away as 800X the length of its body.
If I were a cicada, I could be heard ____ feet away (my height x 800)

A flea can jump 100X the length of its body.
If I were a flea, I could jump ____ feet (my height x 100)

A honey bee can carry up to 1/2 its body weight in nectar and pollen.
If I were a honeybee, I could carry ____ pounds (my weight x .05)

African termites build nests 960X taller than their body length.
If I were a termite, I could build a house ____ feet tall (my height x 960)

[Levels: E/I; Subjects: science/math; Skills: computation/measuring/ visualization]

That Makes Sense. The object of this activity is to help children understand how insect sense the world the world them, and comparing this to the way we do it. Help the children fill in a chart like the following (answers provided):

Sense	Insect Way	Human Way
Touching	(antennae and body hairs)	(skin)
Hearing	(antennae; ear on leg or thorax)	(ears on head)
Seeing	(compound and simple eyes)	(pair of eyes on head)
Smelling	(antennae)	(nose)
Tasting	(antennae or palps near mouth)	(tastebuds on tongue)

[Levels: E/I; Subjects: science/human development; Skills: comparing similarities and differences/critical thinking]

Winging It. To make it easier for children to closely examine insect wings, make some insect wing laminations - sandwich wings between pieces of clear contact paper. You can use already dead insects for this activity. Most transparent and semi-transparent insect wings can be viewed by the group by placing them in standard 35mm slide mounts and projecting them on a screen. Have the children study the patterns made by the wing veins. What geometric shapes or other patterns can they identify? [Levels: E/I; Subject: science; Skills: classification/ comparing similarities and differences/observation]

Insect Vision. One of the distinguishing features of insects are their compound eyes, and children and adults alike are fascinated by the concept of multifaceted vision. Insect vision can be simulated with "fly eye" viewers - which came in a variety of sizes and styles. An insect "eye" can also be from a bundle of 12-20 drinking straws held together with an elastic band. Your activity station can be equipped with a number of these viewers, or the kids can make their own from straws, along with posters explaining how insect eyes work and pictures of real insect eyes. [Levels: P/E/I; Subject: science; Skills: visualization]

How Big is That Bug? This activity is meant to help young bug enthusiasts practice their measuring. Place one or more rulers or measuring scales on a table (attach the rulers with tape, or mark measuring grids right on a paper tablecloth). Have a variety of rubber "bugs" available to be measured. If possible, have a simple worksheet for each child to record the length (and width?) for each type of insect. Help them discover which rubber "bug" is the longest and which is the shortest. You can also compute the average size. [Level: E; Subjects: science/math; Skills: computation/measuring]

Butterfly Wings. Children can make their own set of butterfly wings using an ordinary paper grocery bag. Remove the side of the bag with the seam, and the bottom of the bag, with scissors. Open the bag up and place the logo side down on a table. Draw the body and wings of a butterfly on the plain side; the body of the butterfly should be on the centerline of the bag. Decorate with markers, crayons, tempora paint, construction paper, glitter or other art materials. When complete, have the child try it on and mark where the palm of each hand is located. Make a small vertical slit near each edge so the child can hold the wings across their back and flap their wings. [Levels: P/E; Subject: science/arts; Skills: creativity/drawing/motor skills]

Bug Masks. The kids can make and decorate their own bug masks. If you have it produce it on a card stock the mask will be much more durable. You will need, scissors, crayons, markers, glitter, and string (or elastic) to complete the bug masks. [Levels: P/E; Subject: science/ arts; Skills: creativity]

Bug Antennae. Children can make and wear their very own insect feelers, or antennae. One type uses an inexpensive plastic head band and two chenille strips (pipecleaners). Secure each chenille to the headband with a tight twist. Another type of antennae can be made from aluminum foil. To make this type of antennae, give each child two long (3x12") strips of aluminum foil (construction paper or cardstock could also be used). Have the kids roll and twist the pieces of foil into a headband. Curl two pipecleaners around the headband. The free ends of the chenille antennae can be curled or left straight. If desired you can "segment" the antennae by stacking wooden or plastic beads onto each chenille after they have been attached to the headband. Or, attach a single bead, pompom, or small styrofoam ball at the end of each antenna. [Levels: P/E; Subject: science/arts; Skills: creativity]

Bug Eyes. Styrofoam and cardboard egg cartons can be used as the basis for making a very nice set of insect eyes. Cut the carton into sections, leaving the two adjacent cups intact. Cut holes in the bottom of the cups so that the wearer will be able to see. Attach a chenille at each end of the paired cups (by poking a small hole to put the chenille through), forming a pair of "goggles". Decorate these insect eyes with markers, paint, glitter, aluminum foil, or other materials. [Levels: P/E; Subject: science/arts; Skills: creativity]

Adopt-A-Bug. Set aside some time for the children to observe and describe insects. Pass around an insect (specimen, picture, rubber replica) and have each child say something about the object. You might suggest they look at the physical characteristics (size, shape and color) and, if appropriate, its smell, sounds, and/or feel (textures). Keep a list of all the descriptions on a chart, chalk board, or overhead projector. After the group exercise is complete, give each child an insect (specimen, picture, or rubber replica) and tell them to look carefully at their own adopted "bug" and write a thorough description of it. You might even want to have them draw their own picture of their "adopted" bug. [Levels: E/I; Subject: science/language arts; Skills: comparing similarities and differences/description/drawing/observing/ writing]

Butterfly Alphabet. Have the children look carefully at a collection of butterfly pictures or butterfly specimens and see if any letter or numbers can be found. Levels: P/E/I; Subjects: science/language arts; Skills: observation]

Insect Symmetry. Insects, like humans, have a bilaterally symmetric body shape. At first the children may be intimidated by this big term, but it is easily demonstrated in the following manner. Before your demonstration obtain a 3 foot length of string and tie a weight (washer, button, etc.) on one end. Have one of the children stand facing the group. Hold the string near the middle of their forehead and point out how the string has divided their body into a left and right half. Furthermore, note that just about all visible body parts are paired, or grouped in twos (appear as a "mirror image"); for example, eyes, nostrils,

INSECT WORLD Activity Sheet
Insect Symmetry

Instructions: Insects have a bilaterally symmetric body shape. All this means is that the right half of the body is identical to the left half, and just about all of the body parts come in pairs. Below is a partial picture of an insect. Before you complete the left half of the missing insect, see if you can complete the picture using a mirror. Lay the edge of the mirror along the center line of the insect with the shiny side of the mirror facing right; look in the mirror and you will see a complete insect! Now, use a pencil, pen, crayon, or marker to complete the picture.

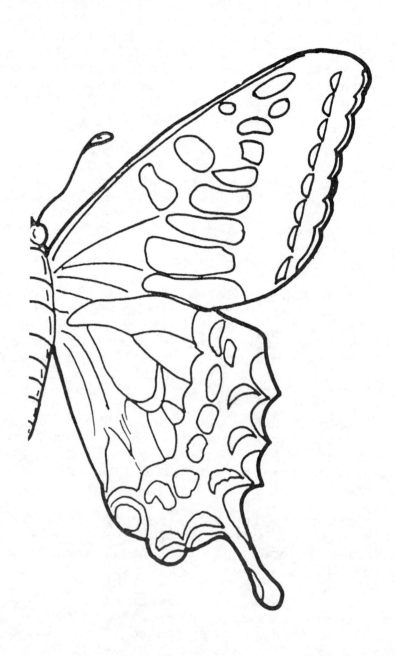

A reproducible resource from "PROJECT B.U.G.S." by Gary A. Dunn, published by the Young Entomologists' Society, Inc., 1915 Peggy Place, Lansing, MI 48910-2553, tel. (517) 887-0499.

ears, arms, legs. (For older children, ask if any of the internal body parts are paired.) Insect bodies are exactly the same: the antennae, eyes, mouthparts, wings, spiracles (breathing pores), and legs are paired. Now pass out the symmetry activity sheet (page 64) and have the children complete the drawing. As an extension of this concept you can easily demonstrate how to complete the activity sheet using a mirror rather than a marker. Place the mirror on its side along the midline of the insect drawing with the mirrored side facing the drawn side. The mirror will recreate the complete insect because both side of a bilaterally symmetric animal body are virtually identical to each other. [Levels: P/E/I; Subjects: science/math/art; Skills: comparing similarities and differences/drawing/observation]

Many-legged Math. Legs and wings can be readily used for calculation exercises: addition, subtraction, multiplication, and division. For example, how many legs in a group of 58 insects? [Levels: E/I; Subjects: science/math; Skills: computation]

References

A Beginners Guide to Observing and Collecting Insects. Gary A. Dunn.
    Young Entomologists' Society. Lansing, MI. 1994.
An Insect's Body. Joanna Cole. William Morrow and Co. New York.
    1984.
Insects and How they Function. Philip Callahan. Holiday House. New
    York. 1971.
What's Inside. Insects. S. Whillock and J. Norsworthy. Dorling and
    Kindersley. New York. 1992.

Lesson 4: HOW INSECTS GROW

Studying the growth and metamorphosis of insects opens the door to understanding how insect bodies function, insect classification, insect behavior, and insect ecology.

Key Points

1. Insects have a life cycle that includes an egg stage, one or more immature stages, and an adult stage. The adults reproduce, and after new eggs are laid, the life cycle starts again.

2. Insects vary in their growth patterns. Most insects change shape as they grow and develop. This change is called metamorphosis. Each of the four types of metamorphosis is associated with one of the four stages of immature stages of insects. Knowing the type of metamorphosis for each group (order) of insects is very important for successful identification, rearing, or pest control. It is generally true that during the insect life cycle it is the immature stage that consumes the most food.

3. Groups of the same insect that live together in a common area are known as a population. The populations of some insects are able to reach incredible numbers in short periods of time.

Activity Ideas

Introducing the Miracle of Metamorphosis. Discuss how insects vary in their growth patterns as compared to other animals. Because they are enclosed within a non-living "shell" they must shed this skeleton in order to grow. Their bodies also change shape as they grow, a process known as metamorphosis. Review the four types of metamorphosis and associate each one with the correct immature stage. They are:

Type of metamorphosis	Name of Immature	Common names
No metamorphosis	young	none
Gradual metamorphosis	nymph	none
Incomplete metamorphosis	naiad	none
Complete metamorphosis	larva	maggot/grub/caterpillar

Life Cycle Sequencing. Obtain copies of inexpensive life cycle books such as "Life Story: Butterfly", "Life Story: Ant" and "Life Story: Spider" by Michael Chinery (Troll Assoc. Mahwah, NJ. 1991.). Carefully remove the pages with the color pictures, laminate each one, and put a strip of velcro "hooks" on the back along the top edge so they can be easily fastened to any feltboard or cloth-covered surface. Now the pictures are ready to be put in the proper sequence by the children (either as a group exercise, or for individual experimentation and practice in your insect learning center). When not in use the pictures can be stored in a pocket next to the felt board. For younger children you may want to provide a solution illustration somewhere nearby. [Levels: P/E/I; Subject: science; Skills: decision making/matching/observing/sequencing]

Insect Life Cycle/Metamorphosis Poster. Have the children (either in small groups or individually) design a poster, using drawings, photographs or actual specimens, which shows either the incomplete or complete metamorphosis of insects they have learned about. [Level: E/I; Subjects: science/arts; Skills: creativity/sequencing/small group work]

Insect Life Cycle Mobile. Draw, color, cut, and assemble into separate mobiles representatives of each life stage of gradual metamorphosis (egg-nymph-adult) and complete metamorphosis (egg-larva-pupa-adult). Hang the mobiles in a prominent place for all to see. Levels: P/E/I; Subjects: science/arts; Skills: creativity/motor skills/ sequencing]

Butterfly Life Cycle 3-D Poster. To help children visualize the metamorphosis of a butterfly, have them make their own 3-D life cycle poster. You will need the following materials: oaktag or other sturdy cardstock for patterns, 8.5x11" piece of tan construction or writing paper, green/red/yellow/orange/purple construction paper, brown tissue paper, dried white peas or beans, and brown/black/green/yellow chenilles (pipecleaners). The children will need scissors, glue, and markers or crayons (optional). If you are going to do this project with younger children you may want to prepare patterns for the leaf and butterfly ahead of time. The illustration below will give you the general idea of what the finished project should look like. Note that there is a green leaf in each quarter of the poster, and that the life stages are in sequential order (starting in the top left corner). The eggs are represented by the white peas, the caterpillar by the chenille piece, and the chrysalis by the crumpled and twisted tissue paper. The butterfly is made from construction paper wings and body. Each of the four steps in the life cycle should be numbered or labeled appropriately. [Level: P/E; Subjects: science/arts; Skills: creativity/drawing/motor skills/sequencing]

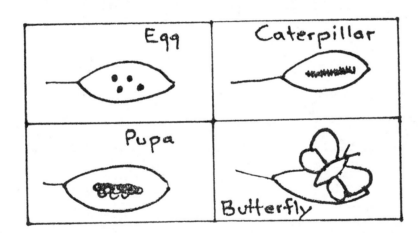

Insect Life Cycle Pyramid Diorama. This special type of diorama correlates the insect life cycle with the seasons, and helps illustrate how insects cope with the changing conditions. The unique feature of this diorama is the pyramidal design which creates four "compartments" or scenes. The background in each scene is decorated with appropriate seasonal colors before being assembled. You will need the following materials: oaktag or other sturdy cardstock for the base, construction paper (green/brown/white/red/yellow/orange/purple), brown tissue paper, dried white peas or beans, and brown/black/green/yellow chenilles (pipecleaners). The children will need scissors, glue, and markers or crayons. Eggs are represented by the white peas, the caterpillar by the chenille piece, and the cocoon by the crumpled and twisted tissue paper. The adult moth is made from construction paper wings and body. Each of the four steps in the life cycle should be numbered or labeled appropriately. [Level: E/I; Subjects: science/arts; Skills: creativity/drawing/motor skills/sequencing]

Insects...

Getting Ready for Winter

Hi! My name is Karl the Caterpillar and I'm getting ready for winter. In the space below please write a story about what happened to me. Thanks.

_____

_____

_____

_____

_____

_____

_____

_____

_____

_____

_____

_____

_____

_____

_____

_____

_____

_____

INSECT WORLD Activity Sheet

Published by the Young Entomologists' Society, Inc., 1915 Peggy Place, Lansing, MI 48910-2553
Phone: (517) 887-0499 Gary A. Dunn, Director of Education. All Rights Reserved.

Metamorphosis Character Sorting. For this activity you will need a collection of insect pictures from magazines, books, calendars, or insect cards (available from the Young Entomologists' Society), and two boxes or bins. Label the bins with one of the following character pairs: gradual metamorphosis/complete metamorphosis or immature/adult. Show each picture and have the children take turns telling which bin the picture should go in. If you relabel the bins you can repeat the activity with the other contrasting character set. [Levels: P/E/I; Subjects: science/human development; Skills: comparing similarities and differences]

Metamorphosis of the Mind. Have the children relax and close their eyes while you read a story about metamorphosis (see references, page 74). Ask the children to imagine that they are the insect character undergoing the activities and changes in the story. Have them describe what they think it would be like to change shape as you grow up. [Levels: P/E/I; Subjects: science/language arts; Skills: listening/visualization]

The Magic Caterpillar. Use a stuffed animal reversible caterpillar/butterfly (available from Y.E.S. and other science suppliers) to illustrate how some insects suddenly change shape as they grow (complete metamorphosis). The caterpillar/butterfly can also be used in combination with "The Very Hungry Caterpillar" by Eric Carle or other similar metamorphosis stories (see references, page 74). [Levels: P/E; Subjects: science/language arts; Skills: listening/visualization]

Live Insects. Several types of insects can be easily raised in the classroom so that children can see the miracle of metamorphosis firsthand. For example, have the children raise mealworms from eggs to adult (mealworms can be obtained from a pet store or bait shop). Place the larvae in screen-covered containers with 1-2" of oatmeal and bran flour. Watch for the pupae and emerging adults (the eggs are very tiny and difficult to find in the food medium). Painted lady butterflies are another easy to rear insect. You can obtain special butterfly life cycle kits for biological supply houses and the Young Entomologists' Society.
   For further suggestions on keeping and raising insects, see page 25. [Levels: P/E/I/; Subject: science; Skills: animal care/small group work]

Imaginary Insect Eggs. You will need enough small (1") rubber "bugs" so that each child can have one. Rubber "bugs" are available from local toy stores, or from the Young Entomologists' Society. Start with several cups of Ivory-brand soap flakes. Add one teaspoon of vegetable oil, and then begin adding small amounts of water until the flakes become mushy and can be shaped by hand. Have each child shape a soap ball ("egg") around their rubber "bug". Set the completed soap balls on wax paper and let them dry until firm. The soap "eggs" can be used for washing until the insect emerges from its egg at a later date. [Level: P/E; Subjects: science/arts; Skills: creativity/motor skills]

Insect Egg Sculptures. Insect eggs come in many sizes, shapes, and textures. They may be round, oval, elongate, flattened, or odd-shaped; they may be smooth or textured with ridges, grooves, bumps, or dimples. Using playdough (commercial or homemade), plasticine, or modeling clay, give children a chance to make an insect egg sculpture. Examples of different insect eggs (adapted from Frost, 1959; Borrow, DeLong and Triplehorn, 1976; Ross, 1956; and Arnett and Jacques, 1985) are given below. You may want to make a large poster of these illustrations for the kids to look at when making their egg models. [Level: P/E/I; Subjects: science/arts; Skills: creativity/motor skills]

INSECT WORLD Activity Sheet
Insect Egg Sculptures

Instructions: Insect eggs come in many sizes, shapes, and textures. Try your hand at making a sculpture of an insect egg. You can make your sculpture out of playdough, Plasticine, modeling clay, wax, plaster, papermache, or even soap. If you really want to get fancy, you could even make ceramic egg models! A few examples of insect eggs are shown below.

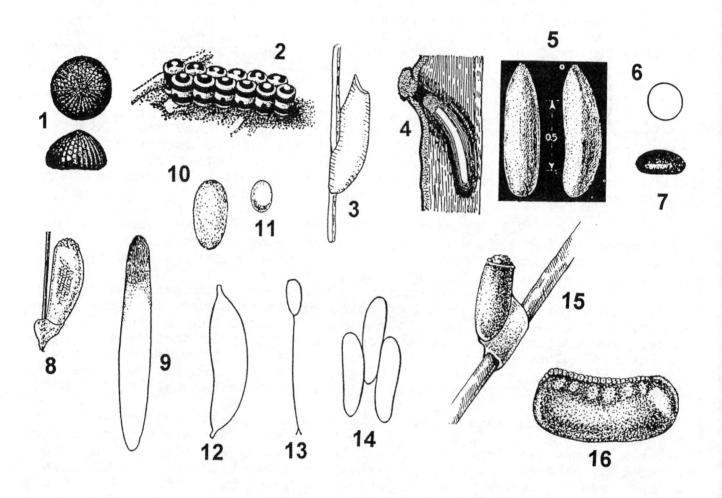

(1) fall armyworm; (2) stinkbug; (3) horse bot fly (on hair); (4) tree cricket (in twig); (5) seedcorn maggot; (6) springtail; (7) aphid; (8) cattle louse (on hair); (9) damselfly; (10) clothes moth; (11) dog flea; (12) ichneumon wasp; (13) lacewing; (14) house flies; (15) head louse (on hair); (16) cockroach egg capsule

A reproducible resource from "PROJECT B.U.G.S." by Gary A. Dunn, published by the Young Entomologists' Society, Inc., 1915 Peggy Place, Lansing, MI 48910-2553, tel. (517) 887-0499.

Hoola-Hoop Bug Count. An ordinary hoola-hoop can be used as a way to count ground-dwelling insects. Have a child toss the hoop down on the ground; then have one or more of the children get down on their hands and knees to look for signs of insect activity over a period of several minutes. This activity works best in areas with herbaceous vegetation (lawns and fields) or leaf litter (wooded areas). Magnifiers may assist in locating tiny insects. Record the type (and number) of insects seen by the insect observers and post the results for all to see. [Levels: P/E/I; Subjects: science/math; Skills: computation/observation]

Bug Census - Estimating Populations. Have you ever wondered how many insects there are in a one acre field? In your backyard? Entomologists often need to know how many insects there are in a crop field, woodland, stream, or other habitat. Since it's often impossible to count every last insect in a large area, entomologists often use estimates (a type of prediction based on a previously established pattern). Learning how to estimate insect populations takes practice. The children can practice counting and estimating insects using small rubber "bugs". To help children practice estimating, obtain a supply of styrofoam meat trays and ziplock plastic bags (slightly larger in dimensions than the meat trays). You will also need a large number of small rubber "bugs". Now you can slide a meat tray into a bag, toss in a varied number of the rubber "bugs", and then zip the bag closed. (You can record the actual count on the bottom of the meat tray if you want to make this exercise self checking.) Later you can practice estimation skills with larger numbers of the rubber "bugs". Allow each child a few moments to look at each tray and right down their guesstimate. Encourage them to practice estimating and not to try making an actual count. [Levels: P/E/I/; Subject: science/ math; Skills: computation/estimation/observation]

Don't Count Your Eggs Before They Hatch. This counting and arithmetic exercise uses an insect theme. You will need a quantity of plastic eggs (like the ones pantyhose come in) and a supply of small (1") rubber "bugs". Fill each egg with an assortment of rubber "bugs", from 1 to 10 in number. Hide the eggs (outdoors or indoors) and let the children search for them. Instruct them not to open the eggs until you say so. As soon as all the eggs are found, gather the children in a circle. Have each child take a turn opening an egg and counting the rubber "bugs" inside. Record the number of "bugs" (by child or by kind of bug) on a chart or blackboard. When all the eggs have been opened, add up the number of insects found by all the children (for really young children you'll need to count the tally, rather than add the numbers). [Levels: P/E; Subject: math; Skills: computation/observation]

How Many Bugs in the Jar? People love guessing games, even buggy ones. Fill a large jar, or even a small dollhouse, with rubber bugs and have the children estimate the number of specimens in the container. You can even tie this activity into insect fecundity. (Did you know one pair of house flies can produce 190,000,000,000,000,000,000 individuals in just 5 months?) First you can allow the children a chance to give their initial guess on the number of rubber "bugs" in the container. Next, challenge the children to device a way to accurately estimate the total number of bugs in the container. [Levels: E/I; Subjects: science/math; Skills: computation/estimation/observation]

INSECT WORLD Activity Sheet
Stamp the Bugs Counting Exercise

Instructions: In the space to the right of each number shown below stamp the same number of insect pictures. If you don't have a set of insect rubber stamps, you can use stickers or make your own drawings. The first one is done for you.

2	🦋 🦋
4	
7	
3	
5	
1	
8	
6	

Keeper of the Bees. A typical queen bee lays over 1000 eggs each day. As a beekeeper you might need to know how your bees are doing, and this is where the children come in. They are going to help the beekeeper keep track of the eggs laid in his 8 hives. Here are the givens: today the queen in Hive "A" laid 1114 eggs; the queen in Hive "B" laid 993 eggs; the queen in Hive "C" laid 976 eggs; the queen in Hive "D" laid 1214 eggs; the queen in Hive "E" laid 1061 eggs; the queen in Hive "F" laid 1028 eggs; the queen in Hive "G" laid 1182 eggs; and the queen in Hive "H" laid 1024 eggs. Here are the questions: What is the highest number of eggs laid by any queen bee? (1214) What is the lowest? (976) What was the total number of honey bee eggs laid today? (8592) What is the average number of eggs laid by these eight queen bees? (1074) Using the average number of eggs laid, on what day will the eight queens have laid 1,000,000 eggs? (on the 117th day) [Levels: E/I; Subjects: science/math; Skills: computation]

Cockroach Math. The German cockroach is one of the most prolific insects on the planet. This is because they have a short life cycle and produce plenty of eggs. Given the following information, see if the children can compute the cockroach population at various points in the future. A female German cockroach often reaches maturity in under 90 days (therefore there may be 4 generations per year). Each female can produce 5 egg capsules during her adult life and each egg capsule contains 35 eggs.

Assuming each baby cockroach that hatches survives to become a reproductive adult, and that half of each generation are male and half are female, what is the population at the end of the first generation, second generation, third generation, etc.? (Solution below)

```
Original population: 2 (1 male, 1 female)
Generation 2: 35 eggs x 5 capsules = 175 cockroaches
Generation 3: (175/2) x 5 x 35 = 15,313
Generation 4: (15,313/2) x 5 x 35 = 1,339,844
- END OF FIRST YEAR -
Generation 5: (1,339,844/2) x 5 x 35 = 117,236,328
Generation 6: (117,236,328/2) x 5 x 35 = 10,258,180,625
Generation 7: (10,258,180,625/2) x 5 x 35 = 897,590,804,688
Generation 8: (897,590,804,688/2) x 5 x 35 = 7.85391954101e+013
- END OF SECOND YEAR -
```

Now recompute the figures using 50% mortality and 90% mortality before maturation (reduce number of breeding females by 50% and then 90%). What is the effect on the population growth? As an extension of this activity, have the children graph the results of their computations to better visualize the population growth. [Levels: E; Subject: math; Skills: computation]

References

Ant (Life Story). Michael Chinery. Troll Assoc. Mahwah, NJ. 1991.

Both Sides Now. Joni Mitchell. Scholastic Inc. New York. 1992.

Butterfly. Moira Butterfield. Simon & Schuster. New York. 1991.

Butterfly (Life Story). Michael Chinery. Troll Assoc. Mahwah, NJ. 1991.

Butterfly (My First Wildlife Book). Keith Faulkner. HarperFestival. New York. 1993.

Butterfly (See How They Grow) Mary Ling. Dorling Kindersley. New York. 1992.

Butterfly and Caterpillar. Barrie Watts. Silver Burdett. Morristown, NJ. 1985.

The Caterpillar and the Polliwog. Jack Kent. Prentice-Hall. New York. 1982.

Caterpillar Caterpillar. Vivian French. Candlewick Press. Cambridge, MA. 1993.

Charlie the Caterpillar. Dom DeLuise. Simon & Schuster. New York. 1990.

Dragonfly. Barrie Watts. Silver Burdett Press. Englewood Cliffs, NJ. 1988.

From Egg to Butterfly. Marlene Reidel. Carolrhoda Books. Minneapoils, MN. 1974.

Honeybee. Barrie Watts. Silver Burdett Press. Englewood Cliffs, NJ. 1989.

How Insects Grow. Gladys Conklin. Holiday House. New York. 1969.

Insect Metamorphosis: From Egg to Adult. Ron and Nancy Goor. Atheneum. New York. 1990.

Insects and their Young. Ross E. Hutchins. Dodd, Mead and Co. New York. 1975.

Ladybug. Barrie Watts. Silver Burdett Press. Morristown, NJ. 1986.

Life Cycle of a Butterfly. M. Linton and T. Terry. Bookwrights Press. New York. 1988.

Life Cycle of the Butterfly. Paula Z. Hogan. Raintree Publishers. Milwaukee, WI. 1979.

Life Cycle of the Honey Bee. Paula Z. Hogan. Raintree Publishers. Milwaukee, WI. 1991.

Metamophosis. Patricia Quiri. Franklin Watts. New York. 1991.

Moth (Stopwatch Book.) Barrie Watts. Silver Burdett Press. Englewood Cliffs, NJ. 1990.

Two Lives. Joyce Pope. Raintree Steck-Vaughn. Austin, TX. 1992.

The Very Hungry Caterpillar. Eric Carle. Philomel Books. New York. 1979

Where Do They Go? Insects in Winter. Millicent Selsam. Scholastic Inc. New York. 1982.

Lesson 5: Insect Classification and Identification

Now that the children can recognize an insect (distinguish them from other animal groups), and their major body parts, the next step is learning to distinguish between different types of insects. At first, stick to the prominent, well-known insect groups such as the beetles, butterflies and moths, ants, bees and wasps, flies, true bugs, and grasshoppers, crickets and their relatives. A few of the smaller insect groups are also easily recognized, for example, dragonflies, earwigs, and fleas.

Identifying insects beyond the order level can be both a fun and challenging experience. Fortunately, there is a wealth of resources available to assist you and your group (see reference at end of chapter).

Key Points

1. Classification is an aid to identification. The categories of scientific classification are kingdom, phylum, class, order, family, genus, and species.

2. Insects are classified, divided into groups, based on various body and developmental characteristics. Most simple classification centers around the orders, which are the largest groupings of similar insects.

3. Listed below are the most significant orders of insects. The major orders are given in bold type; 90% of the insects are in these 7 groups.

Order name	Common name or examples	Metamorphosis	Mouthparts	Wings
Thysanura	silverfish/firebrats	simple	chewing	0
Collembola	springtails	simple	chewing	0
Orthoptera	grasshoppers/crickets	gradual	chewing	0-4
Blattodea	cockroaches	gradual	chewing	0-4
Mantodea	mantids	gradual	chewing	2
Phasmatodea	stick & leaf insects	gradual	chewing	0-4
Dermaptera	earwigs	gradual	chewing	4
Ephemeroptera	mayflies	incomplete	none	4
Odonata	dragonflies/damselflies	incomplete	chewing	4
Plecoptera	stoneflies	incomplete	chewing	4
Isoptera	termites	gradual	chewing	0-4
Mallophaga	chewing lice	gradual	chewing	0
Anoplura	sucking lice (human lice)	gradual	sucking	0
Psocoptera	booklice/barklice	gradual	chewing	0-4
Thysanoptera	thrips	gradual/complete	sucking	0-4
Hemiptera	true bugs	gradual	sucking	4
Homoptera	aphids/scale insects/ hoppers/mealybugs/cicadas	gradual	sucking	0-4
Neuroptera	lacewings/antlions/dobsonflies	complete	chewing	4
Coleoptera	beetles/weevils	complete	chewing	0-4
Mecoptera	scorpionflies	complete	chewing	4
Trichoptera	caddisflies	complete	sponging	4
Lepidoptera	butterflies/moths/skippers	complete	siphoning	4
Diptera	flies/gnats/midges/mosquito	complete	sucking	0-2
Siphonaptera	fleas	complete	sucking	0
Hymenoptera	sawflies/ants/bees/wasps	complete	chewing	0-4

Consult one of the insect field guides listed at the end of this lesson if you need more information on the metamorphosis, mouthparts, wings, and special body structures for each of these insect orders.

4. A classifying tool known as a "dichotomous key" is used to sort insects by common features and determine the correct identification. These keys are created by experts who have studied the classification of a certain insect groups.

Activity Ideas

Animal Kingdom Sorting Board. For this activity you will need a large felt-covered board and some animal pictures or drawings (featuring a mixture of molluscs, worms, reptiles, amphibians, arthropods, birds, and mammals). Each of the animal pictures can be photocopied onto colored paper (and then laminated or mounted on foamcore board for durability). You will also need three other signs: 1) I AM NOT AN INSECT, 2) I AM AN INSECT, and 3) PICK AN ANIMAL AND PLACE IT WHERE IT BELONGS. Attach small pieces of Velcro (hooks, not loops) on the back of all the animal pictures and the heading signs.

Place the three heading signs near the top of the felt board, starting with "PICK AN ANIMAL AND PLACE IT WHERE IT BELONGS" on the left third, and "I AM NOT AN INSECT" and "I AM AN INSECT" on the right two-thirds. Randomly arrange the pictures beneath the sign on the left and challenge the children to "classify" the animals by placing them under the proper sign on the right. Periodically remove the animals so that the sorting board can be used throughout the day as free time permits. [Levels: E/I; Subjects: science/language arts; Skills: analysis/communication/decision making]

Which Doesn't Belong Here? You can easily put together a worksheet of animal, arthropod, and insect pictures to test the childrens ability to identify the individual that doesn't belong to the set. Each set of four animals would have three that belong to the set (three arthropods or three insects) and a fourth that doesn't belong (a non-arthropod animal or a non-insect arthropod). For example:

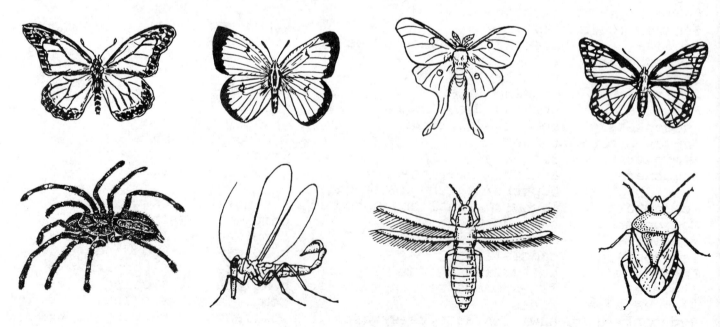

Are Your Orders in Order? Have the children give examples of insect orders and some of the insects in each order. You might try the "insect alphabet", naming an insect beginning with the letter "A" (antlion), "B" (butterfly), etc. Have the children place the insects in the proper group (order). also, write questions about the insect orders on 3x5 cards, or slips of paper. Place the questions in a container and have each child draw a slip of paper and then answer the question. Questions could include the following:

- Which order has the largest number of insects? (beetles/Coleoptera)
- How does the Hemiptera differ from the Homoptera? (type of wings)
- What insect order has scale-covered wings? (butterflies and moths/Lepidoptera
- Are the butterfly, caddisfly, and horse fly in the same order? (No: butterfly=Lepidoptera, caddisfly=Trichoptera, horse fly= Diptera)
- What order is characterized by one pair of wings and halteres? (true flies/Diptera)
- Are the lightningbug, ladybug, and bed bug in the same order? (No: lightningbug and ladybug=Coleoptera, bed bug=Hemiptera)
- Name an insect order that has aquatic immatures (beetles/Coleoptera, true bugs/Hemiptera, stoneflies/Plecoptera, mayflies/ Ephemeroptera, caddisflies/Trichoptera, true flies/Diptera
- Name an insect order that has chewing mouthparts? (grasshoppers and crickets/Orthoptera, earwigs/Dermaptera, dragonflies and damselflies/Odonata, chewing lice/Mallophaga, beetles/ Coleoptera, or lacewings/Neuroptera)
- Name an insect order with gradual metamorphosis. (grasshopper and crickets/Orthoptera, earwigs/Dermaptera, termites/Isoptera, chewing lice/Mallophaga, sucking lice/Anoplura, true bugs/Hemiptera or cicadas, aphids, and hoppers/Homoptera)
- What insect order is characterized by hemelytra? (true bugs /Hemiptera)
- Name an insect order with members that can sting (ants, bees and wasps/Hymenoptera)

[Levels: E/I; Subjects: science/language arts; Skills: communication/ vocabulary]

Insect Order Sorting. Insects are classified into orders based upon similarities and differences in body characters and life cycles, especially number and type of wings, antennae, metamorphosis, mouthparts, and body shape and unique structures. If you have a collection of insects and/or arthropod pictures these can be used to practice sorting insects/arthropods into their respective groups (see chart on page 75). Of course it is also possible to use specimens from a real insect collection for sorting insects into their correct orders (if you have access to a collection). For more information on collecting insects, see page 17. [Levels: P/E/I; Subject: science; Skills: classification/ comparing similarities and differences/interpretation/recognition/ vocabulary]

Rubber Bugs and Identification. If you don't have real insects, or choose not to use real insects, you can still give children a chance to practice insect identification by using rubber replica insects and arthropods. If you are unable to find suitable rubber or plastic replicas locally, the Young Entomologists' Society can supply a wide variety of different types at an affordable cost (send for free catalog). Have the children (singly or in small groups) spread the insects out on a table or desk and look for ways to sort the insects into their respective orders by studying the body parts that are visible and arranging them according to similarities they find. Most good replicas can be identified using the same keys designed for real insects; or, in the reverse process the children can use the specimens to create their own identification key. [Levels: E/I; Subject: science; Skills: application/classification/ comparing similarities and differences/decision making/interpretation/ observation/reading/recognition/small group work/vocabulary]

Insect Order Matching Exercise. You can easily create a matching exercise by listing insect names (common name or scientific name, depending on the age of the children) on one side of a sheet of paper, and insect illustrations (clip art, rubber stamp art, or stickers) on the other side. An example is included in this book on page 19. A reusable matching exercise can be made by running the activity sheet with list of names and illustrations through a laminator. Water-based markers (overhead transparency pens) can be used to draw lines from the names to the pictures. [Levels: E/I; Subject: science; Skills: application/ classification/comparing similarities and differences/decision making/ interpretation/observation/reading/recognition/vocabulary]

Insect Order Venn Diagrams. A Venn diagram is simply a circle that encloses a group of things (insects in our case) that have something in common (mouthparts, metamorphosis, or wing type in our case). When two or more sets contain some of the same members, their circles overlap. Of course, sometimes objects are left that do not fit any set and form a set by themselves. Children can experiment with Venn diagrams by using string loops and rubber "bugs", or drawing lines around pictures on paper. A reusable Venn diagram exercise can be made by applying stickers (or rubber stamps or pictures) to a sheet of paper, and then running it through a laminator. Water-based markers (overhead transparency pens) can be used to draw lines from the names to the pictures. [Levels: E/I; Subject: science; Skills: application/classification/comparing similarities and differences/decision making/interpretation/observation/reading/ recognition/vocabulary]

The Mystery Insect. Provide each child with a name or picture of an insect. Instruct them not to show their name or picture to the others. Randomly select one child to be the first mystery insect. Have the other children ask questions that can be answered with either a yes or no response to discover the identity of the mystery insect. For example, "Does your insect have wings?" (Mystery insect answers "yes" or "no", depending on the insect he/she has.) Continue until somebody guesses the correct identity of the "mystery" insect. This person becomes the next mystery insect. Continue until everyone has been the mystery insect. [Level: E/I; Subjects: language arts/science; Skills: communication/ critical thinking/decision-making/interpretation/listening/vocabulary]

Insect Order Puzzles. You can easily create a wide variety of crossword and wordfind puzzles using the common and scientific names of insect groups. A variety of inexpensive computer software/shareware is available to make this job easier. Two examples to get you started are included in this book (see pages 81 and 82). [Levels: E/I; Subjects: science/language arts; Skills: vocabulary]

INSECT WORLD Activity Sheet
Who Are We?

Can you find our pictures below? Match the insect picture to the correct name. (Write the letter in the space to the right of the name, or draw a line from the name to the picture.) The answers are given at the bottom of the page. No peeking!!

1. **Rhinocerus beetle** __
2. **Harlequin bug** __
3. **Moth** __
4. **Grasshopper** __
5. **Scale insects** __
6. **Scorpionfly** __
7. **Praying mantis** __
8. **Yellowjacket** __
9. **Butterfly** __
10. **Camel cricket** __

Answers: rhinocerus beetle-F, harlequin bug-J, moth-B, grasshopper-E, scale insects-D, scorpionfly-I, praying mantis-G, yellowjacket-A, butterfly-H, and camel cricket-C

A reproducible resource from "PROJECT B.U.G.S." by Gary A. Dunn, published by the Young Entomologists' Society, Inc., 1915 Peggy Place, Lansing, MI 48910-2553, tel. (517) 887-0499.

Find the Insect. Try taping a small selection of large insect cut-outs to the walls or floors. Play music for the children to move to. When the music stops, announce the name of an insect group, and they can run and touch a picture of an insects from that group. [Levels: P/E; Subjects: science/human development; Skills: decision making/ identification/listening/observation/vocabulary]

Many Names for the Same Insect. Around the world many different words are used as the names for common insects. Have the children conduct an investigation into the names of insects in other languages. For younger children you may just want to share some of the more interesting names with them. A list of some of the more simple insect names are given below. [Levels: E/I; Subject: language arts; Skills: vocabulary]

ENGLISH	GERMAN	FRENCH	SPANISH	ITALIAN
ants	ameisen	formicides	hormiga	formica
bees	bienen	apoides	abeja	ape
beetle	kafer	coleopteres	escarabajo	colleottero
butterfly	schmetterlinge	papillon	mariposa	farfalla
cicada	zikaden	cigales	cigarra	
cockroach	schaben	blatte	cucaracha	blatta
crickets	grillen	gryllides	grillo	grillo
fleas	flohe	puces	pulga	pulce
flies	zweiflugler	dipteres	mosca	mosca
grasshoppers	feldheuschrecken	acridiens	saltamontes	cavalletta
insects	insekten	insectes	insecto	insetto

Insect Art Gallery. Make a poster, bulletin board, or "insect art gallery" of insect pictures highlighting insect shapes, sizes, and colors. Coloring sheets (part of the "Insect Fun Pak) are available from Y.E.S. (send for a free catalog). Have the children draw their own pictures, or collect pictures from magazines, pesticide sales literature, extension publications or other sources. [Levels: P/E/I; Subjects: science/arts; Skills: creativity/drawing]

The Bug of the Day. For this activity you will need a collection of insect pictures (from old magazines, calendars, etc.) and a homemade "television/computer monitor" template. Construct a mock TV screen or computer monitor out of cardboard or other sturdy material (see figure). Label the front of the "monitor" with the words "Insect of the Day". Attach a plastic sleeve to the back of the "monitor" so that it forms a

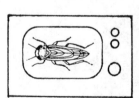

pocket into which you can slide a picture of an insect. Give the children most of the day to study the picture, and at some point later in the day ask for a volunteer to identify the insect (order, family, and common name, if possible). Change the picture on a daily basis. [Levels: P/E/I; Subjects: science/arts; Skills: identification]

Bug Quiz Bulletin Board. You can make a classroom or hallway bulletin board into a giant matching exercise. On the left side of the board arrange a series of insect pictures, each with a letter. On the right side of the board arrange a list of insect names, each with a number. On the bottom right hand corner place the answers beneath a folded piece of construction paper. (1. Ladybug = D, etc.) For variety you can expand on this idea to feature other arthropod groups, or to feature specific insect orders (e.g., just beetles families). [Levels: E/I; Subject: science; Skills: identification/matching/observation]

INSECT WORLD Activity Sheet
Insect Name Wordfind

Instructions: There are nearly 100,000 different kinds of insects that occur in North America. The names of 30 common insects are hidden in the wordfind puzzle below. Can you find them? The names you are looking for include grasshopper, dragonfly, cricket, walkingstick, termite, butterfly, cockroach, mayfly, silverfish, booklouse, stonefly, mosquito, bug, aphid, ant, scale, beetle, cicada, earwig, mantis, lacewing, honeybee, thrips, scorpionfly, caddisfly, louse, moth, wasp, locust, and fly. The names may be up-and-down, across, or diagonal; some are even backwards! Good luck!!

```
S  U  S  Y  L  F  N  O  I  P  R  O  C  S  M  Y
D  I  A  T  N  G  E  C  E  L  A  A  E  F  A  W
E  L  L  Y  N  H  R  S  N  L  C  E  C  B  Y  A
B  E  T  V  S  A  C  A  U  S  T  I  Y  U  F  S
H  A  B  E  E  I  D  A  S  O  C  E  C  G  L  P
C  M  C  Y  R  R  T  B  D  S  L  A  E  A  Y  I
A  O  R  N  E  M  F  N  U  D  H  K  L  B  D  A
O  S  I  M  E  N  I  I  A  T  I  O  O  E  T  A
R  Q  C  O  L  I  O  T  S  M  T  S  P  O  L  E
K  U  K  T  A  T  Q  H  E  H  Y  E  F  P  B  W
C  I  E  H  L  A  C  E  W  I  N  G  R  L  E  C
O  T  T  O  E  S  T  O  N  E  F  L  Y  F  Y  R
C  O  K  C  I  T  S  G  N  I  K  L  A  W  L  D
E  S  U  O  L  C  Y  L  F  N  O  G  A  R  D  Y
U  D  I  H  P  A  Y  L  F  A  L  O  C  U  S  T
I  A  F  A  E  A  R  W  I  G  S  P  I  R  H  T
```

A reproducible resource from "PROJECT B.U.G.S." by Gary A. Dunn, published by the Young Entomologists' Society, Inc., 1915 Peggy Place, Lansing, MI 48910-2553, tel. (517) 887-0499.

INSECT WORLD Activity Sheet #22
Are Your Orders in Order?

Instructions: Complete the crossword puzzle using the clues given below. (Hint: Use common names.)

ACROSS

1. A hardworking Hymenoptera.
4. A Diptera that bites us, but fish like to bite them!
6. Dainty green or brown aphid munching Neuropterans.
8. The most common insects are the Coleoptera.
10. You know Dermapterans don't really crawl in folks ears, don't you?
11. Eating wallpaper paste suits the Thysanura just fine.
13. A short life dancing over the water is all the Ephemeroptera enjoy as adults.
14. Some sting, some are parasites, but all are Hymenoptera.
16. Colorful flower visitors, we can call the Lepidoptera.
17. Trichoptera build houses of gravel in the streambed.
19. Aerial acrobats after mosquitoes, Odonata have been at it a long time.
20. This Hymenoptera has been called the most valuable insect to man.

DOWN

2. A funny name for a strange insect some call Thysanoptera.
3. A True Hemipteran
5. Aquatic as nymphs, the Plecoptera fly to lights as adults.
7. Some of these Homopterans only visit every 17 years or so.
9. Isoptera aren't welcome in anyone's house!
11. Collembola these primitive insects are called.
12. Not a fly nor an arachnid, its the order Mecoptera.
15. Small Homoptera that cause trouble in the garden.
18. Siphonoptera might make your dog or cat itch.

A reproducible resource from "Insect World", published by the Young Entomologists' Society, Inc.,
1915 Peggy Place, Lansing, MI 48910-2553, tel. (517) 887-0499. Puzzle by Bill O'Donnell, Eminence, MO

Bug Bingo. This game is a big hit every time. This game is played in the same manner as the traditional bingo game, but the bingo cards feature insects or insect-related items rather than numbers and letters. There are various ways to play the "buggy" version of bingo. All you need are bingo cards, markers or game chips, and a spinner or container with the insect/item names. If you don't want to take the time to create your own game materials, three different Bug Bingo kits are available from the Young Entomologists' Society for a nominal fee (send for free catalog). [Levels: P/E/I; Subject: science; Skills: identification/matching/ observation]

What Bug Am I? Divide the group into teams of 4 to 6 children. Assign each group one of the following insects: dragonfly, grasshopper, termite, butterfly, bee, ant, mosquito, true bug, mayfly, mantis, beetle, earwig, moth, walkingstick, cockroach, or flea. Each team should write down 10 clues about their insect, and arrange them from least specific to most specific. Have each team read their clues and see how long it takes others to guess the identity of the group's insect. [Levels: P/E/I; Subjects: science/language arts; Skills: description/identification/ observation/writing]

Who Am I? Tape a picture on the back of each child. On a signal each child finds a partner (or two) and asks questions about his/her identity. The questions must be answerable with a yes or a no. For example, "Do I have one pair of wings?" or "Are my antennae long?" Instead of an ice-breaker activity, this activity can also be set up in a gameshow format. Levels: E/I; Subject: science; Skills: classification/ critical thinking/communication]

Who Am I Quiz. This activity can be run as a live presentation with verbal clues given to the audience, or as a self-service activity station using a quiz board (see page 114) or picture and/or clue cards with flipup answer panels. The Smithsonian Insect Quiz (available from Y.E.S. and other science suppliers) is an exceptional source of information for this activity, or you can create your own clues.

Here are some sample clues:
We hop in the grass, so we're called _____. (Answer: grasshoppers)
She's not your sister or your mother, but she's married to your father's
   brother. (Answer: "ant")
I have a brother for a dragon and I'm a "lady" who likes to fly near
   streams. (Answer: damselfly)
People disagree in calling me a beetle, bug, or bird, but they all call me
   a lady. (Answer: ladybird beetle or ladybug)
My cousin is a bumbler, and she's busy too, but she won't make honey for
   you. (Answer: honey bee)
I'm happy and sing with all my might, especially on a warm summer night.
   (Answer: katydid)
I don't like butter and I'm not really a fly. (Answer: butterfly)
Our mining trails show up in leaves like shiners, we mine in leaves so
   we're called _____. (Answer: leafminers)
You might think he's religious because of his attitude of prayer, but
   don't be fooled by this hungry fellow, insects beware! (Answer:
   praying mantis)
We'll bite you too if you wish, but deer and horses are our main dish.
   (Answer: horse or deer fly)
I am the best dressed insect I am told, with wings of green and eyes of
   gold. (Answer: lacewing)

I can cause crop damage beyond belief, I'm a homopterous insects that hops
     from leaf to leaf. (Answer: leafhopper)
We fly at night and you might not like our hum, and if you're unprotected
     we're really bothersome. You don't like us, but we think you're
     sweet; we suck your blood and think it's a treat. (Answer: mosquito)
Our house has many shapes like bubbles, cones and balls, a style of house
     we call _____. (Answer: galls)
Some of us are good and some of us are bad, but that doesn't make any of
     us sad; to protect ourselves we make a big stink, and that's really
     clever don't you think? (Answer: stink bugs)
I'm a very long insect from aft to fore, and I eat tree leaves - pass me
     some more! (Answer: walkingstick)
On cold winter nights I sing by the chimney and hope for a visit from my
     great cousin Jiminy. (Answer: cricket)
[Levels: P/E/I; Subjects: science/language arts; Skills: critical
thinking/description/identification/listening]

     Insect Dominoes. There are commercially available versions of
insect dominoes, but it's really easy to make your own set. All you need
are wood blocks (cut from molding or other suitable pine wood) and insect
pictures. The insect pictures can be hand drawn or applied with rubber
stamps; or, use insect stickers. For a jumbo sized set of insect
dominoes, use the Insect Cards (available from the Young Entomologists
Society) glued to pieces of 1x4" lumber. For added durability, all
dominoes should be treated with at least two coats of a clear
polyeurethane finish. [Levels: P/E/I; Subjects: science/child
development; Skills: comparing similarities and differences/matching/
observation]

     Concentration Cards. You will need a set of matched playing cards
for this game. You can make your own set or use the special "Insect
Cards" available from Y.E.S. and other science suppliers. Each player
turns over two cards at a time, looking for a match. If the cards match
they are removed from the game. Play continues until all the cards have
been picked up. For variety the matches can be picture/picture (two adult
insects or immature/adult insect) or picture/word. [Levels: P/E/I;
Subjects: science/child development; Skills: matching/observation]

     Insect Flashcards There are no ready-to-use insect flash cards on
the market at this time, but it's not difficult to make your own set of
insect flashcards You can use the special "Insect Cards" (with names
removed) available from the Young Entomologists' Society and other science
suppliers. They can also be made from pictures gathered from old nature
magazines, calendars, and brochures, or you can use insect stickers or
rubber stamps (available from Y.E.S. and other suppliers). [Levels:
P/E/I; Subjects: science/child development; Skills: identification/
matching/observation]

     More Card Games. Let the children play the Hidden Kingdom rummy or
other nature card games, available from teacher and nature stores or the
Young Entomologists' Society, to learn more about insect identification
and relatiopnships. [Levels: P/E/I; Subjects: science/child development;
Skills: critical thinking/matching/observation]

     All Mixed Up.   You can easily make your own homemade insect
"jigsaw" puzzles out of pictures gathered from old nature magazines,
calendars, and brochures. Cut the pictures into different geometric
shapes. For added durability you can mount the pictures on cardboard or

laminate them before cutting. Give the children lots of opportunities to assemble the mixed up puzzle pieces, and name the different insects. [Levels: P/E/I; Subjects: science/child development; Skills: critical thinking/matching/observation]

Our Own Field Guide. Have the class develop a "field guide" to 30+ species of commonly encountered, easily recognized insects. Include complete descriptions and information on their natural history (life cycle, seasonality, habitat, interactions with other animals and plants, etc.), and a picture or drawing, if possible. Have the class decide how to arrange the pages (by color, by insect group, or by habitat). If you use a looseleaf notebook or scrapbook you can add more insects each year. [Levels: E/I; Subjects: science/language arts; Skills: critical thinking/communication/drawing/identification/observation]

Describing a New Species. Thousands of new species of insects are described each year. The insect scientist must write a thorough description that includes all the physical characteristics (size, shape, color, etc.), habits, and life cycle information. Fill a container with a mixture of rubber "bugs". Have each child reach in and pick one out. Give each child 15-20 minutes to write a detailed description of their "new" species. The description should be detailed enough, that if read to the rest of the group they should be able to figure out what it is. Extensions: add a drawing; make up a scientific name and common name; make up information on geographic distribution and habits (food, etc.). [Levels: E/I; Subjects: science/language arts; Skills: critical thinking/ communication/creativity/description/drawing/writing]

References

The Audubon Society Field Guide to North American Insects and Spiders.
    Lorus and Marjory Milne. A.A. Knopf. New York. 1980.
Butterflies and Moths. R.T. Mitchell and H.S. Zim. Golden Press.
    Racine, WI. 1987.
Butterflies and Moths (Eyewitness Handbook). David Carter. Dorling
    Kindersley. New York. 1992.
Butterflies Through Binoculars. Jeffrey Glassberg. Oxford University
    Press. New York. 1993.
Familiar Insects and Spiders. John Farrand Jr. A.A. Knopf. New York.
    1988.
**A Field Guide to the Butterflies of North America East of the Great
    Plains.** Paul Opler. Houghton Mifflin. Boston. 1992.
A Field Guide to the Beetles of North America. Richard White.
    Houghton Mifflin. Boston. 1983.
A Field Guide to the Moths of Eastern North America. Charles Covell,
    Jr. Houghton Mifflin. Boston. 1984.
A Field Guide to the Insects of America North of Mexico. Donald Borror
    and Richard White. Houghton Mifflin. Boston. 1970.
How to Know the Aquatic Insects. Dennis Lemkuhl. William C. Brown Co.
    Dubuque, IA. 1979.
How to Know the Grasshoppers, Crickets, Cockroaches and Their Allies.
    Jacques Helfer. Dover Publ. Co. New York. 1987.
How to Know the Insects. Roger Bland and H.E. Jacques. W.C. Brown.
    Dubuque, IA. 1978.
How to Know the True Bugs. J.A. Slater and R.M. Baranowski. William C.
    Brown Co. Dubuque, IA. 1978.

The Insect Identification Guide. Gary A. Dunn. Young Entomologists'
  Society. Lansing, MI 1994.
Insect Pests. G.S. Fichter and H.S. Zim. Golden Press. Racine, WI.
  1987.
Insects. H.S. Zim and C. Cottam. Golden Press. Racine, WI. 1987.
Insects (American Nature Guides). George C. McGavin. Smithmark
  Publishers. New York. 1992.
An Instant Guide to Butterflies. Pamela Forey and Cecilia
  Fitzsimmons. Bonanza Books. New York. 1987.
An Instant Guide to Insects. Pamela Forey and Cecilia Fitzsimmons.
  Bonanza Books. New York. 1987.
Invertebrate Zoology. Real Kids, Real Science. Ellen Doris. Thames
  and Hudson. New York. 1993.
No Bones. Elizabeth Shepherd. Macmillan Publ. Co. New York. 1988.
Peterson First Guides: Insects. Christopher Leahy. Houghton Mifflin.
  Boston. 1987.
Peterson First Guide to Caterpillars. Amy Bartlet Wright. Houghton
  Mifflin. Boston. 1993.
Pond Life. George K. Reid. Golden Press. Racine, WI. 1987.
The Practical Entomologist. Rick Imes. Simon & Schuster. New York.
  1992.
Simon and Schuster's Guide to Insects. Ross H. Arnett and Richard
  Jacques, Jr. Simon & Schuster. New York. 1981.
Spiders and their Kin. Herbert and Lorna Levi. Golden Press. Racine,
  WI. 1990.

Lesson 6: Insect Behavior

Insects do many strange and amazing things. Learning about insect behavior will help you understand why insects do what they do, and how it helps them survive in the natural world.

Key Points

1. Behavior is the outward, visible activities of insects. Insect behavior requires a stimulus, an urge to satisfy a special need.

2. Insects have three basic needs that determine almost all of their behavior: (a) sustenance (finding food), (b) survival (remaining alive) and (c) reproduction (finding a mate).

3. Behavior is one of the ways that insects adapt to their environment. Insects have many ways of sensing changes in their environment and of responding to those changes. Behavior is one adaptation that helps insects respond to their environment and to become more successful.

4. Insects are adapted to their environments. Adaptations are inherited attributes or features that enable insects to carry out their life functions and survive in the natural world. Adaptations include physical structures (size, shape, and special body features), as well as internal processes (egg production, food digestion and protection against hazards). Insects have adaptations for breathing, feeding, escaping enemies, sensing changes in the environment, and mating.

Activity Ideas: INSECT COMMUNICATION

Flight of the Bumblebee. Play "Flight of the Bumblebee" and have the children pretend to fly around the room and dance like a busy bumblebee. Of course it's also appropriate for bees to buzz as they fly! The children may enjoy making props or costumes (tin-foil/pipe-cleaner antennae and cardboard wings; see the lesson on insect body parts). [Levels: P/E; Subjects: science/arts; Skills: creativity/motor skills]

The Katydid Quartet. Try communicating insect style. Prepare sets of cards (3+ cards per set) that have katydid/grasshopper names and songs on them (each katydid has a different song: true conehead katydid - katy-did-katy-she-did; robust conehead - ze, ze, ze, ze, ze, ze; sword-bearing conehead - tick, tick, tick, tick; Coulee cricket - chip, chip-chip, chip; angular winged katydid - tzeet, tzeet, tzeet; fork-tailed katydid - zeep, zeep, zeep; slender meadow grasshopper - tip, tip, tip, tsee; agile meadow grasshopper - zip, zip, zip, zee; common meadow grasshopper - zee-e-e-e--ee, zee-e-e-e-ee; and black field cricket - chir-r-up). Distribute cards with katydid cards to the children. See if the children can find the other katydids of the same species by calling out their songs (some songs can also be made by using combs and pencils). [Levels: P/E/I; Subjects: science/arts; Skills: communication/ creativity/ motor skills]

The Living Thermometer. Catch crickets (or purchase crickets at a local pet shop) and place them in a small screen cage you can move around. Place the cage in different areas with different temperatures, and record how many chirps it makes per 1/4 minute (15 seconds) at different temperatures. Use a thermometer to determine the temperature. Make a graph of your data. Put degrees on one scale and number of chirps on the other. At some later time when the cricket is chirping, count the number of chirps per 15 seconds and see if you can predict what the temperature is.

The chirp rate for the snowy tree cricket is the most predictable and has been shown to fit the following formula: number of chirps in 15 seconds + 40 = temperature ($^{\circ}$F). This can lead to some interesting math problems. For example, what is the temperature if the cricket chirps 19 times during a 15 second interval? Or, if the temperature is 75°F, how many chirps can you expect to hear in 15 seconds? [Levels: E/I; Subject: science; Skills: charting and graphing/communication/computation/creativity/measuring/motor skills/prediction]

A Flash in the Dark. Observe some fireflies to study their flash patterns. Are the flash patterns the same for each species? Why are they different? Can you imitate the flash patterns with a flashlight? If you have access to a darkened room free of furniture, have the children imitate firefly communication using flashlights. Divide the group into several small groups, each with its own unique flash pattern, and then see if the individuals of each group can find each other (without speaking, of course). [Levels: E/I; Subject: science; Skills: communication/observation/visualization]

Acting Like Insects. Have the children try acting out some different types of insect behaviors, like the bee dance, pheromone trails and scents, social colonies, or food selection.

The behavior of the honey bee is certainly one of the most fascinating types of insects (animal!) behavior. Like other social insects, honey bees live in societies whose survival is dependent upon mutual cooperation and a division of labor. Each colony consists of a single queen (reproductive female), many workers (non-reproductive females), and a few drones (reproductive males). Let the children pretend to be honey bees! Construct a make-believe "hive" by positioning some desks or chairs in a circle, with a small break in the circle serving as the entrance. A queen bee is designated (the teacher?) and two children are assigned to the jobs of guards (keep intruders out) and cleaners (make and maintain the cells and brood); four to six children can be assigned to the job of foragers (search for food). Other children are designated as flowers (and some are given a small supply of nectar and pollen (yellow balloons, tennis balls, or pompoms). One worker leaves the nest and locates a flower with nectar and pollen, returning to the nest with these valuable materials. The returning forager performs the waggle dance, a figure-eight pattern with the straight run ("waggle") directed towards the source of the nectar and the "flowers". The rest of the "foragers", armed with the directional information supplied by the waggle dance, now leave the "hive" to gather more of the valuable nectar and pollen.

Having the children make props or costumes (tin-foil/ pipe-cleaner antennae and cardboard wings) adds immensely to the quality of the role-playing. You can use the poems from a book like "Joyful Noise: Poems for Two Voices" by Paul Fleischman as scripts for role playing insect behavior. [Levels: P/E; Subjects: science/arts; Skills: creativity/motor skills]

Smart Termites. Here is a fascinating demonstration of termite behavior. You will need a piece of writing paper, a <u>Papermate</u> brand pen, and some live worker termites. Use the pen to write your name (or any word) on the paper in large cursive letters. Now place the termites on the paper. The termites will align themselves with the ink trail, making it look like they are "reading" what you have written. Ask the children if they can explain what is happening. (The ink used by the Papermate Pen Co. contains chemicals similar to the trail marking pheromones of the termites!) Incidentally, the same type of demonstration can be given using ants and a solution of formic acid (applied with a quill pen or cotton swab. [Levels: P/E/I; Subject: science; Skills: hypothesizing]

Activities: <u>PROTECTIVE COLORATION</u>

The Great Indoor Moth Hunt. Have the children trace and cut out appropriately sized moth outlines on plain white paper. Using crayons, markers, pens, pencils or watercolors, camouflage the outlines to look like the surfaces in the classroom. Using tape, mount the "moths" on walls, wastepaper baskets, desks, etc. and invite a guest (or another group) to find as many of the moths as he/she/they can in one minute. Discuss how camouflage is an important survival method. How many moths were not seen? Help the guest locate the remaining moths. [Levels: P/E/I; Subject: science; Skills: observation/visualization]

The Walkingstick Jungle. If you want to do a similar exercise outdoors, make walkingstick insects out of pipecleaners (a variety of bright and earth-tone colors). Place the stick insects along an outdoor trail in plain sight (on vegetation and the ground). Have the children walk down the trail and look for the hidden "walkingsticks". Instruct the children to keep their sightings to themselves and not to help other children. Have each student keep track of the number of "walkingsticks" they see. How many "walkingsticks" did each child see? What color(s) were the hardest to see? [Levels: E/I; Subject: science; Skills: observation/visualization]

Aphid Alley. Spray paint dried lima beans a variety of colors: bright orange, yellow, green, blue, and tan. Take a known number of the lima bean "aphids" (50 or more, with an equal number of each color) and scatter them on the ground in an area of barren soil and short vegetation. Give a small group of children ("the ladybugs") 30 seconds to collect as many of the "aphids" as possible. Have each child count the number of each color "aphid" they collected. Which color(s) were found most frequently? (and why?) [Levels: P/E/I; Subject: science; Skills: observation/visualization]

TIP: Even if you can't go outdoors to try these camouflage exercises, try it indoors. Make a mock habitat using pieces of different textured and colored fabrics (old carpeting works well).

Critter Search. Fill and dish pan or other tray with two to three inches of oatmeal (or sawdust). Mix in a variety of small rubber "bugs" so that they cannot be seen on the surface. Use a mixture of bright and earth-tone colors. Give each child one minute to search through the oatmeal or sawdust in search of "bugs". Chart and graph the results for each child in the group. Which colors were collected most frequently? Least frequently? Have the children discuss and explain the results of their critter search. [Levels: P/E/I; Subject: science; Skills: observation/motor skills/visualization]

Many Types of Camouflage. Study insect camouflage by looking for the ways that insects use their coloration or body shape to avoid their enemies or fool their prey. Look for insects that resemble (a) twigs (walkingsticks), (b) thorns (treehoppers), (c) tree bark (many moths), (d) green leaves (mantid), (e) the color of a flower, (f) buds or bumps on twigs (scale insects), or (g) has spots that look like the eyes of a larger animal (many butterflies and moths). Make a record of your observations with notes, collections, photographs or videos. How do these traits help these insects? [Levels: E/I; Subject: science; Skills: communication/critical thinking/observation/prediction/visualization]

Protective Coloration. Using pictures of insects or actual specimens, look for insects that are brightly colored in alternating stripes of black and yellow, black and orange, or black and red. What "messages" are insects giving to other animals through these color patterns? Discuss how certain colors are used to give information. For example, what warning colors do people use? (red and white = stop, black and yellow road sign = danger). [Levels: P/E/I; Subject: science; Skills: communication/critical thinking/prediction]

Activities: LOCOMOTION AND MOVEMENT

Insect Broadjump. How far can an insect jump? Make an insect jumping arena by drawing a series of concentric circles (at measured distances) around a central point. Place an insect on the center point and record the distance of the jump. Compute the minimum, maximum, and average jump for each individual of a species. Compare different species. Measure the height of each child and give them several chances at broad jumping as far as they can. Relate the height of each child to the length of their jump. (Most children will only be able to jump a distance that is less than their height.) Do the same for the grasshoppers. Who can jump farther (when compared by relative size)? (Hint: grasshoppers are known to jump up to 80 times their body length!) [Levels: E/I; Subjects: science/math; Skills: communication/computation/critical thinking/prediction/small group work]

Racing Insects. There's no betting allowed at these races! You can use either mealworms, crickets, bessbugs, or cockroaches as miniature race horses (without riders). Use a cardboard disk (like the ones pizzas come on) as the racetracks. To get ready for the race have each participant put their insect in a small cup. Place the cardboard circle on top of the cup and then invert the cup and circle together. Gently slide the cup to the center of the circle. On a signal, each participant (or team) lifts their cup to release the insect; the first insect to reach and fall off the edge of the circle is the winner. Another variation is to put several insects on one "racetrack" and have people guess which one is going to win (mark each with a spot of paint). The use of a bright spotlight (bulb with aluminum reflector) over the center of a circular racetrack or at the starting end of a linear racetrack will speed the insects up.
To increase the educational value of this activity, it's a good idea to talk for a few moments about the insects being used. [Levels: E/I; Subjects: science/math; Skills: communication/computation/critical thinking/ prediction/small group work]

How Fast Can an Insect Run? Make an insect running arena by drawing a series of concentric circles (at measured distances) around a central point. Place an insect on the center point and record the time of the run. Compute the minimum, maximum, and average speed (in inches or centimeters per minute) for each individual of a species (and possibly different species if you have time). (You may want to convert the inches/centimeters per minute to miles per hour.) Compare different species. As a variation to this experiment, place some of the insects in a jar and refrigerate them for 15 minutes, and time them again. After 15 minutes time them again. Next gently warm them with an electric light (or the sun), and time them again. What effect does temperature have on the activity of insects? [Levels: E/I; Subjects: science/math; Skills: communication/ computation/critical thinking/prediction/small group work]

Jumping Beetles. Have the children search for a click beetle (several species if possible). Place the click beetles on their back and watch how they turn over. How are the beetles able to do this? How high can they jump? Have the children imitate the click beetles actions. [Levels: E/I; Subjects: science/math; Skills: communication/computation/ critical thinking/prediction/small group work]

Activities: SURVIVAL, ADAPTATION, AND EVOLUTION

Make An Insect Fossil. Help the children make their own insect fossil replicas. Place a dead insect into an inverted bottle cap. Drip clear nail polish (or casting resin) onto the insect until it is completely covered. Let it dry. Repeat the process until 5 or 6 layers of polish have been applied. The insects now looks like it has been preserved in amber (petrified tree sap!).
A different type of fossil can be made by pressing an insect specimen (rubber replicas or galls would work best) into clay or wet plaster to make a "negative" (reverse) impression. It is now possible to make a "positive" impression from the negative. First coat the negative casting with a thin layer of salad oil or petroleum jelly. Then make a ring of thin cardboard and place it around the insect impression. Mix more plaster of Paris and pour it over the coated impression. Let it set until hardened; take off the ring and gently separate the two halves of the casting. There is your fossil replica! [Levels: E/I; Subjects: science/ art; Skills: modeling]

Winter Wonderland. Find out where different insects spend the winter, and in what life stage. What common insects overwinter as eggs, immatures, pupae, or adults? Examples of overwintering insects that can be found include: moth pupae (in sandy soil near trees and shrubs and under rotten logs), praying mantids (egg masses on weeds), silk moths (cocoons on trees and shrubs), tent caterpillars (egg masses on twigs or cherry and crabapple), grasshoppers (eggs in soil), mourning cloak butterfly (adult butterfly in rotten trees and logs). (See INSECT WORLD 1(6):1-2 for more information.) [Levels: E/I; Subject: science; Skills: critical thinking/observation/research]

What's For Dinner? Have the children gather and present information on the food habits, life cycle, and habitat of an insect that interests them. Have them explain how knowing this information would be helpful to a collector or observer. [Levels: E/I; Subject: science; Skills: critical thinking/observation/research]

Monarch Migration. Discuss why it is important for monarch butterflies to migrate (as a tropical butterfly they cannot overwinter in northern parts of the USA and Canada). On a map of North America, locate and mark your home town. Locate Zitacuaro (Michoacan/Mexico border 50 miles west of Mexico City) if you live east of the Rocky Mountains, or Pacific Grove, California if you lives west of the Rocky Mountains. What is the shortest distance between your hometown and the appropriate overwintering sites? What geographical obstacle(s) are in the way? Prepare a "flight plan" - if you travel 50 miles per day, how long do you predict it will take you to get there.

Are there other butterflies that migrate? Yes - painted lady, snout butterfly, and some sulphurs/whites. What are some of the "political" problems for an animal that crosses international borders? [Level: E/I; Subjects: math/science; Skills: computation/critical thinking/measuring/ map skills/]

Become a Monarch Tagger. Your group can become a part of the worldwide network of monarch taggers that are helping to unravel the remaining mysteries about monarch migration. Order your tags and information at least six to eight weeks in advance. The fall (southward) migration generally begins in late August in the northern regions, and three to four weeks later in more southern areas. The spring (northward) migration from Mexico begins the last week in February. Write to the following: (1) Insect Migration Studies, University of Toronto-Scarborough Campus, 1265 Military Trail, Scarborough, Ontario M1C 1A4, CANADA; (2) Don Davis, 3815 Bathurst Street Apt. 2, Downsview, Ontario M3H 3N1, CANADA; or (3) The Monarch Program, P.O. Box 178671, San Diego, CA 92177. [Level: E/I; Subject: science; Skills: application/communication/small group work]

Wasp Nest Dissection. Because the large gray nests of the yellowjackets and baldface hornets and the small paper nest of the paper wasps are abandoned at the end of each season, they can be safely collected in the late fall and early winter (after several heavy frosts). Closely examine the exterior of the nest - what color is the paper and why? (same color as the bark of the local trees, from which the paper is made) Where is the entrance hole to the nest? (generally near the bottom apex, slightly off to one side) How was it attached to the plant or other object? Using scissors, carefully remove 1/3 to 1/2 of the outer paper to expose the inner nest structure. How many layers of outer paper are there, and why? (extra insulation; also provide places of the adults to reside) How many "stories" are there to the larval cells? How many larval cells are there? Did all the larvae complete their development? This would also be an excellent opportunity to discuss how and why social Hymenoptera (bees and wasps) defend themselves and their nests. [Levels: P/E/I/; Subjects: science/math; Skills: computation/ critical thinking/interpretation/observation]

Papermaking. Did you know that insects are the actual inventors of paper? Paper wasps and hornets have been making paper for millions of years. It was the ancient Egyptians that noticed this behavior and came up with their own version of paper (known as papyrus). You can use old newspaper (a 12 x 12" square should be plenty) as your raw material for making new paper (just like the wasps use tree bark). Cut the paper into strips, and then into small squares. Place these pieces in a large bowl and add one cup of warm water. Let the paper soak for a little while. Once the paper is wet and soft you can begin the process of "pulping" it by churning the paper/water with an electric mixer (or better yet an old blender). Keep this up until the paper is broken up into oat-size pieces. Now you must add a binder to glue the paper pieces back together once they begin to dry. A tablespoon of wallpaper paste or starch such be dissolved in a small amount of water, and then added to the pulp (continue the mixing for awhile longer). Now pour the pulp onto a screen (a removable windowscreen will do just fine - it won't be damaged) so that the excess water can be removed. It's a good idea to suspend the screen over a cake pan or some absorbent newspapers. Spread the pulp out on the screen in a thin layer. To speed up the drying process, place a piece of wax paper on the pulp and roll a jar or rolling pin over it to squeeze out some of the water. Carefully remove the wax paper and let the air do the rest. When completely dried, the new paper can be peeled off of the screen. [Levels: P/E/I; Subject: science; Skills: visualization]

Imaginative Insect Interviews. Divide the group into teams of two. In each group one child will be the "insect" (designated by you) and the other will be the "bug reporter". Together they can decide on a few questions to be asked on the life cycle, habits, and behavior of the "insect" during a special "interview". After sufficient time to prepare, have each team conduct their interview in front of the whole group. You can even equip the reporter with a fake microphone. (If the names of the insects to be interviewed are kept a secret it would be possible to make this a "mystery guest" situation where the audience figures out the identity of the insect from the answers to the questions.) [Levels: E/I; Subjects: language arts/science; Skills: creativity/public speaking/ research]

Hercules or Weakling? Conduct a study to determine the strength of an insect. How much weight can an insect lift? Prepare a weight lifting table for the insects. Test different insects (individuals and species) by adding weights to the container at the end of the string (and don't forget to add in the weight of the container and string). Does the table's surface texture affect the insect's ability to pull ("lift") the weight? Compute the average and maximum weight lifting ability for each species. [Levels: P/E/I; Subjects: science/math; Skills: computation/ critical thinking/experimentation/interpretation/invention/observation]

Behavior of Aquatic Insects. Collect a variety of aquatic insects (and plants) and place them in an aquarium set up to resemble a natural aquatic habitat. Make notes on the insect activity. How do they get air? What do they feed on? How is it that some aquatic insects can walk on the water, but other terrestrial insects cannot? (See next activity.) [Levels: P/E/I/; Subject: science; Skills: critical thinking/ interpretation/observation/writing]

Walking on Water. How do water striders and other aquatic insects walk on the surface of the water? To demonstrate how this is possible, fill a water glass or beaker with water. Place a small piece of tissue paper (1-2 inches square) on the surface of the water and then carefully place a sewing needle on the tissue paper. What happens to the needle when the tissue paper sinks? Any other observations? What happens if the tip of the needle breaks the surface film? Now examine the feet of a water strider? What are they like? Where is the claw? Why? [Levels: E/I; Subject: science; Skills: critical thinking/hypothesizing/ observation]

Antlion Antics. Make a portable sand-filled box to house antlion larvae (also known as doodlebugs). Feed them a variety of small insects, especially ants, and watch how the larvae trap their prey. Keep notes on the number and kinds of insects eaten. [Levels: E/I; Subject: science; Skills: observation/writing]

References

Amazing Animal Disguises Sandie Sowler. A.A. Knopf. New York. 1992.

Animals that Build Their Homes. Robert M. McClung. National Geographic Society. Washington, DC. 1976.

Animals that Glow. Judith Presnall. Franklin Watts. New York. 1993.

The Architecture of Animals. Adrian Forsyth. Camden House. Camden East, Ontario. 1989.

Backyard Insects. Millicent Selsam and Ronald Goor. Four Winds Press. New York. 1981.

Bugs for Dinner? Sam and Beryl Epstein. Macmillan Publishing Co. New York. 1989.

Camouflage: Nature`s Defense. Nancy Warren Ferrel. Franklin Watts. New York. 1989.

Chirping Insects. Sylvia Johnson. Lerner Publishing Co. Minneapolis, MN. 1976.

Communication Among the Social Bees. Martin Lindauer. Atheneum. New York. 1967.

Crickets and Katydids, Concerts and Solos. Vincent Dethier. Harvard University Press. Cambridge, MA. 1992.

The Evolution Book. Sara Stein. Workman Publishing. New York.

The Evolution of Insects. Philip Callahan. Holiday House. New York. 1972.

Experiments with Animal Behavior. Ovid K. Wong. Children's Press. Chicago. 1988.

Exploring the World of Insects. Adrian Forsyth. Firefly Books. Willowdale, Ontario. 1992.

Exploring the World of Social Insects. Hilda Simon. Vanguard Press. New York. 1962.

Extinct Insects and Those in Danger of Extinction. Philip Steele. Franklin Watts. New York. 1992.

Find the Hidden Insect. Joanna Cole and J. Wexler. William Morrow and Co. 1979.

A Guide to Observing Insect Lives. Donald Stokes. Little, Brown and Co. Boston. 1983.

Hidden Messages. D. Van Woerkom. Crown Publishers. New York. 1979.

How Insects Communicate. Dorothy Hindshaw Patent. Holiday House. New York. 1975.

How to Hide a Butterfly. Ruth Heller. Grossett and Dunlap. New York. 1985.

Incredible Insect Instincts. Paul Mirocha. Harper Collins. New York. 1992.

Insect Behavior. Philip Callahan. Four Winds Press. New York. 1970.

Insect Builders and Craftsmen. Ross Hutchins. E.M. Hale and Co. Eau Claire, WI. 1959.

Insect Communities. Ernestine Noorsgaard. Grossett and Dunlap. 1973.

Insect Masquerades. Hilda Simon. Viking Press. New York. 1968.

Insect Travelers. John Kaufman. William Morrow and Co. New York. 1972.

Insect Worlds. Lorus and Marjory Milne. Charles Scribner's Sons. New York. 1980.

Insects and the Homes they Build. Dorothy Sterling. Doubleday and Co. Garden City, NY. 1954.

Insects and their Homes. Hidetomo Oda. Raintree Publishers. Milwaukee, WI. 1986.

Insects Build Their Homes. Gladys Conklin. Holiday House. New York. 1972.

Insects that Live Together. Michael Dempsey and A. Sheehan. World Publishing Co. New York. 1970.

Insects: Seasons in their Lives. Beverley Wallace. Bobbs-Merrill Co. Indianapolis, IN. 1975.

Insects: Their Secret World. Evelyn Cheesman. Apollo Editions. New York. 1952.

Katydids - The Singing Insects. Barbara Ford. Julian Messner. New York. 1976.

Living Fossils: Curious Creatures. Joyce Pope. Steck-Vaughn. Austin, TX. 1992.

Mistaken Identity. Joyce Pope. Steck-Vaughn Publishers. Austin, TX. 1992.

Musical Insects. Bette J. Davis. Lothrup, Lee and Shepard. New York. 1971.

Nature's Light - The Story of Bioluminescence. Francine Jacobs. William Morrow and Co. New York. 1974.

Nature's Pretenders. Alice Hopf. G.P. Putnam's Sons. New York. 1979.

Nature's Tricksters. Mary Batten. Little, Brown and Co. Boston. 1992.

Poisonous Insects. (First Sight.) Lionel Bender Gloucester Press. New York. 1988.

Poisonous Insects. (Picture Library.) Norman Barrett. Franklin Watts. New York, NY. 1991.

Read About Insects that Live in Families. Dean Morris. Raintree Publishers. Milwaukee, WI. 1988.

The Social Insects. O.W. Richards. Harper and Bros. New York. 1960.

Social Life in the Insect World. J.H. Fabre. The Century Co. New York. 1914.

Vanishing Animal Neighbors. Geraldine Gutfreund. Franklin Watts. New York. 1993.

Where's That Insects? Barbara Brenner and B. Chardiet. Scholastic, Inc. New York. 1993.

Lesson 7: Ecological Studies of Live Insects

The many ways in which insects interact with other insects and animals, plants, and the environment (ecology) is one of the most fascinating aspects of insect life. Since the objective here is to observe and study insects in their natural environment, most of these activities require going outside where the insects can be observed in the act of being themselves. However, a few ecological processes (such as predation, population dynamics, and response to changes in the environment, for example) can be demonstrated under controlled laboratory conditions.

Key Points

1. As the largest group of animals on the planet, insects play many vital roles in ecological systems - as pollinators, members of the food web, and decomposers/recyclers. Insects have a significant effect upon other animal species, plant life, and the environment.

2. Many interesting facts about insect ecology can be discovered by observing insects in their natural habitat.

Activity Ideas

Bugs for Dinner. Have the group make a list of all the animals (and plants!) that eat insects. This can be done individually, in small groups, or by the group as a whole. Once your list is as complete as you can get it, have each children draw a picture of their favorite insect-eater; or, perhaps they can help you collect pictures of insect-eaters from old nature magazines, calendars, or wildlife brochures. To complete the discussion, you will need to make a list of the things that insects eat, and the animals that eat insect-eaters. Now you can easily show who different animals and plants depend upon one another.

Once you have a good collection of drawings or pictures you can demonstrate a 3-D food pyramid by attaching each illustration to a "building block" (made from a small cardboard box) that can be stacked with the plants/soil/compost on the bottom, the insects above this, the insect-eaters above this, and the large carnivores at the top. With this type of demonstration it is easy for the children to see how each group depends on the group below it.

Similarly, you can demonstrate a food web with your picture collection and a ball of yarn. Give each child a picture of a food web component (sun, plants, decomposers, insects, insect-eaters, and large carnivores) and form the group into a large circle. Hand the ball of yarn to the "sun"; have the "sun" hold onto the loose end of the yarn and toss the ball to one of the plants. The idea is to connect organisms that need each other in some way (as food, pollinators, decomposers, carbon dioxide or oxygen sources, etc.). Keep tossing the yarn until all the possible environmental, plant and animal interactions have been connected. Levels: E/I; Subjects: science: Skills: interpretation/visualization]

Bats and Moths. In Austin, Texas there is a colony of 5 million bats that live under the Congress Avenue Bridge. Each night these bats consume 60,000 pounds - 30 tons - of moths (and other insects) each night! Here is a game that 15 to 30 children can play to demonstrate the nighttime interaction of bats and moths. The only materials you need are four to six blindfolds and pictures of a bat and a moth (but these are not absolutely essential). Assemble the group into a circle and have them hold hands. Hold up the picture of the bat and explain to the group that bats are flying mammals that eat insects. However, they cannot see the moths very well at night and so they use use high-pitched (ultrasonic) sound waves to locate the moths. Now hold up the picture of the moth and explain that moths are night-flying insects that are out searching for food. They use their antennae to hear and avoid the moths. Now hold up both pictures and shout "The bat eats the moths!" (If you like you can have the group chant this a few times to get everybody ready to play. Select one child to be the first bat (and apply the blindfold). Move this child to the center of the circle and tell them that when play starts they must say "bat, bat, bat" all of the time. Select the first of the moths and apply the blindfolds to them. Likewise they should be instructed to say "moth, moth, moth" all of the time. The object of the game is for the moths to avoid capture at all costs. Have the rest of the group join hands and remind the bat and moths that they must stay in the ring at all times. To start the game yell (what else) "The bat eats the moths!" When a moth gets grabbed, it goes an joins hands in the circle. Choose the new "bat" from among the better "moths", and then select a new set of "moths". Play until everyone has had a chance to participate or grows tired of the game. (Game concept by Dr. David L. Evans.) [Levels: P/E/I; Subjects: science/child development; Skills: motor skills/visualization]

Insectivorous Plants. Take a field trip to a bog to find and observe insect-eating plants such as pitcher plants, sundews and Venus' flytraps. You may also want to set up an indoor terrarium that includes pitcher plants, Venus' flytraps or sundews (purchased from a plant store).

Pond Community. A pond is an ideal community to study because it is a small ecosystem in itself. All of the plants and animals that inhabit the pond are specialized for an aquatic existence. Of course, it also goes without saying that kids love to "muck around" at the edge of a pond.
    After you locate a suitable pond, choose a warm day for your excursion to the pond. (Although aquatic insects are active year round, it's risky to work around water in cool or cold weather). You will find the following items useful for pond studies: dip net (kitchen strainer), white pan or tray, assorted jars and bottles, magnifiers, waterscope (see below), thermometer, forceps and eyedroppers, field guides, and a notebook. You can attach a long handle to your dipper, and scoop insects out of the pond without getting unduly soaked. Place the contents of each scoop in the white pan and sort through the muck and vegetation to locate the insects. A specially designed Pond Study Kit is available from Y.E.S. (send for a free catalog) that contains everything you need to conduct successful pond studies. Like any habitat study, keep notes on the types and numbers of insects found and what they were doing. You may also want to keep a few of the live insects and plants to stock an aquarium so that you can have your own indoor "pond" community. [Levels: P/E/I; Subjects: science; Skills: identification/listing/mapping/motor skills/observation]

Window on the Water World. Make a waterscope for viewing aquatic insects. Cover one end of a metal cylinder (an old juice can will do nicely) with clear cellophane wrap. Hold the cellophane in place with waterproof tape or elastic bands. To use the waterscope, put the cellophane end into the water and look into the scope! [Levels: E/I; Subject: science; Skills: observation]

INSECT WORLD Activity Sheet
Pond Study Data Sheet

Instructions: Take this Pond Study Data Sheet along with you on your next trip to a local pond. Circle the plants and animals that you observe. You may wish to make other notes on the back of this sheet, such as observations on preferred habitats for each animal/plant, habits and behavior, daily or seasonal activities and/or abundance. Use a different sheet for each pond you visit. Also, if you cover both sides of this Pond Study Data Sheet with clear contact paper you can write on it with erasable markers (and it will be waterproof).

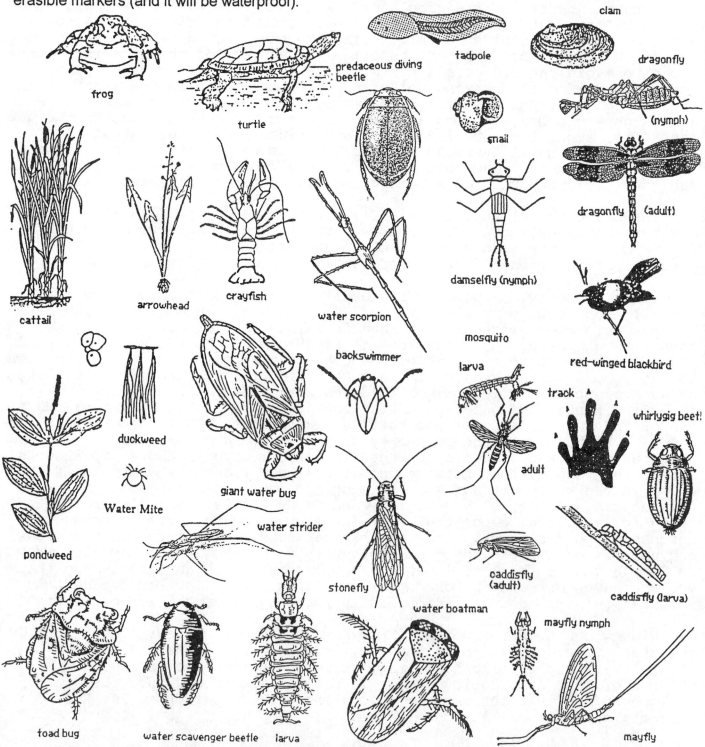

frog

turtle

predaceous diving beetle

tadpole

clam

snail

dragonfly (nymph)

dragonfly (adult)

cattail

arrowhead

crayfish

water scorpion

damselfly (nymph)

mosquito

red-winged blackbird

duckweed

Water Mite

giant water bug

backswimmer

larva

track

adult

whirlygig beetl

pondweed

water strider

stonefly

caddisfly (adult)

caddisfly (larva)

water boatman

mayfly nymph

toad bug

water scavenger beetle

larva

mayfly

A reproducible resource from "PROJECT B.U.G.S." by Gary A. Dunn, published by the Young Entomologists' Society, Inc., 1915 Peggy Place, Lansing, MI 48910-2553, tel. (517) 887-0499.

Watching Insect and Plant Interactions. Choose a plant that attracts a number of insects (goldenrod, Spirea, milkweed, wild carrot, for example) and record the activity and number of insects that you find on an individual plant or in a patch of plants. Be sure the children check the foliage, flowers, and woody portions of the plant. How does the activity differ at various times of the day or season? In addition to taking notes, it is also possible to take photographs, or even videos of insect activity. [Levels: E/I; Subjects: science/ language arts; Skills: estimating/identification/listing/observation]

Leafminer Leaf Laminations. Leafmining insects make interesting leafmine patterns in leaves of many types of plants. You can collect and save examples of interesting leafmines with a simple technique. All you need is some clear contact paper, note paper, a pen or pencil, and scissors. You will get the best results with this techniques if you make your leaf laminations as soon after picking the leaves as possible.

Cut a piece of contact paper that is bigger than the leaf you plan to laminate. Peal the backing from the contact paper and place it face down (sticky side up) on a table. Hold the contact paper by the edges so you don't get fingerprints and smudges all over the center of the contact paper. Now, place the leaf face down on the contact paper and lightly press it down. Make a label for your lamination that includes the city/town and state where the leaf was collected, the date the leaf was collected, the name(s) of the collector(s), and the name of the plant (if known). Place this label face down next to the leaf. Cut a second piece of contact paper about the same size as the first (don't worry if they're not exactly the same size).

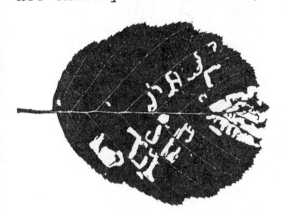

Peel the backing off of the contact paper and carefully press it down on the leaf and label. It helps if you stick down the middle of the second piece of contact paper first, and then press and smooth the contact paper from the center outward towards the edges. If you get any large air bubbles under the contact paper, poke a small hole in the bubble with a needle and smooth the spot down. Now you can trim off the edges and make the lamination nice and square (or rectangular, as the case may be). Now you will be able to enjoy the leafmine pattern for a long time to come. [Levels: P/E/I; Subject: science/arts; Skills: observation]

This Way, Honey. Many flowers have special color patterns to direct bees to the nectar. Some of these patterns, typically consisting of stripes, help guide the bees to the center of the flower where the nectar is located. Some unicolorous flowers also have elaborate patterns, but they are invisible to the human eye under natural light. To locate these "hidden" honey guides, place the plant under an ultraviolet (UV) blacklight in a darkened room. Set up a trial to discover which common plants have honey guides and which do not. [Levels: E/I; Subject: science; Skills: experimentation/observation/prediction]

The Insect Inn. Dead trees are important to many animals, including many species of insects. As the tree goes through various stages of decomposition, each stage provides different conditions and attracts different insects. Some insects use the dead trees as shelter, and hide under loose bark or the tunnels of other insects. The insulating powers of the bark and wood protect many insects from the extremes of summer and winter temperatures. Some insects feed on the wood, and actually

participate in the decomposition of the wood. Other insects are predators
and parasites and are there to search for their prey or hosts. If you can
locate one or more dead trees (hopefully in various stages of
decomposition), you and your children can easily observe insects as they
use this "insect inn". Make notes of your observations. What insects do
you see? Why are they there? What part of the dead tree are they using?
[Level: E/I; Subject: science; Skills: listing/interpretation/observation]

Butterfly Gardening = Butterfly Habitat. Nothing is more rewarding
than the establishment or maintenance of a beautiful butterfly garden. In
addition to gaining insight into butterfly behavior, it will also provide
an opportunity to explore related topics such as seeds, plant care, soils,
plant identification, and small garden animals. To make a butterfly
garden a reality you will need a garden site, plants, access to water, and
gardeners. The children can easily participate in many aspects of the
garden construction and maintenance. Some "Butterfly Garden Guidelines"
may be helpful: (1) listen when someone is talking; (2) follow directions
the first time they are given; (3) if you have questions, stop, ask, then
go on; (4) use care in handling tools; (5) take turns and work
cooperatively with others; (6) treat plants gently; (7) please do not
throw dirt and no playing with the water; (8) paths are to walk on; (8)
garden is for the butterflies and other animals; (10) enjoy and have fun.

A great deal of information on planning, designing, and planting
butterfly gardens has been written in books and magazine articles (see the
references at the end of this chapter), so it will not be discussed here.
However, the children can assist in coming up with a list of butterflies
that can reasonably be expected to occur in the area, and lists of
suitable nectar plants and larval food plants. Before the garden is
planted, take the time to conduct a survey of the kinds and numbers of
butterflies that occur in the area. Later, after the garden is
established, you can repeat your survey. Perhaps you will want to graph
the results.

Other additions to your garden might be a butterfly feeder (filled
with sugar water, and fruit scraps), hibernation boxes, and a small
butterfly watering hole (plastic-lined depression two to three feet in
diameter, six to eight inches deep in middle, with small rocks on the edge
and in the shallows). [Levels: P/E/I; Subject: science; Skills:
application/charting and graphing/communication/cooperation/
identification/listening/listing/mapping/measuring/problem solving/
research/small group work]

Habitat Analysis. Plan a field trip to two or three different
habitats (You can probably do this right on or near the school
property.) Before you get there, ask the children to predict what types
of insects they think they will find in each different type of habitat.
Have the group develop a list of the insects they catch (or see) within
each habitat and compare with their predictions. You might also want to
prepare a graph of the number of different insects found in each habitat
type. This will help answer the question "which habitat has the greatest
diversity of insects?" For tips on locating insects in their natural
habitats, see "A Beginner's Guide to Observing and Collecting Insects" by
Gary A. Dunn (Young Entomologists' Society. Lansing, MI. 1994.)
[Levels: E/I; Subjects: science/math; Skills: charting and graphing/
critical thinking/identification/interpretation/listing/mapping/
observation/small group work]

Habitat Mapping. Help the children make a map of your community upon which they can identify insect habitats and some of the common insects seen there. This map does not need to be elaborate, and can be a simple sketch map (see below). Your map will make it easier to relocate areas of interest, like special habitats and places you have collected. These maps will also help you record the changes that take place in the area over the years.

Maps are not that difficult to make. Whenever possible, the map should be drawn to scale (e.g., 1 inch equals 1 mile), but this is not absolutely necessary. However, north should always be located at the top of the map. Sketch in the primary man-made and natural features like roads, towns, railroads, streams, and lakes. Then, add in other useful reference points and landmarks (buildings, fences, prominent trees, hills, etc.). Don't forget to label as many of these features as you can. You should also put the date on the bottom of the map, for future reference. Now you can identify areas with interesting insect habitats. [Levels: E/I; Subjects: science/social studies; Skills: creativity/mapping/visualization]

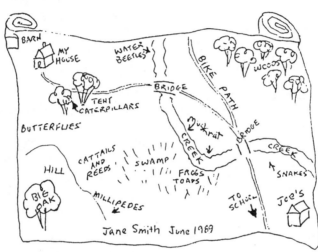

Hoola-Hoop Bug Count. An ordinary hoola-hoop can be used to help study the diversity and numbers of ground-dwelling insects. This investigation can be done individually or in small groups. To establish a study plot, have a child toss the hoop down on the ground; then have one or more of the children get down on their hands and knees to look for signs of insect activity. This activity works best in areas with herbaceous vegetation (lawns and fields) or leaf litter (wooded areas), but it may also be interesting to contrast the results from different types of habitats (including "barren" soil). Magnifiers may assist in locating tiny insects. Record the names, numbers, and ecological role (plant feeder, predator, or decomposer) of insects seen by the insect observers and post the results for all to see. Have the children look for any interactions between plants and plants, plants and insects, insects and insects, plants and environment, and insects and environment. It might also be a good idea to draw a map of the study plot, marking down any significant features such as large rocks, bare spots, clumps of plants, etc. [Levels: P/E/I; Subjects: science/math; Skills: computation/observation]

Micro World. Read the story "If I Were an Ant" by Amy Moses (Childrens Press. Chicago. 1992.), "If You Were an Ant" by Barbara Brenner (Harper and Row. New York. 1973.), or "Step by Step" by Diane Wolkstein (Morrow Junior Book. New York. 1994.). This should get the children thinking about the large objects that insects encounter on a

daily basis! Give each child a piece of string about 3 feet long and then
lead the group outdoors. Have each child choose a spot in an open area
and have them lay their string down on the ground. Have them get down on
their hands and knees and follow the string "trail". What types of
obstacles do they run into? What other creatures do they encounter on
their journey? Are they able to locate food and shelter on their "trip"?
When you return indoors, younger children can draw a picture about their
imaginary "micro-journey", while the older children can write a short
story based on their observations (complete with "map" and drawing?).
[Levels: P/E/I; Subjects: language arts/science/arts; Skills:
communication/creativity/ mapping/observation/writing]

Insect Life List. Help the children, either individually or as a
group, maintain a list of insects seen for a single locality (schoolyard
or nearby park). For each sighting be sure to record the date, the name
of the insect(s), what the insect(s) was/were doing, and name(s) of the
observer(s). A large wall chart is ideal for this activity. After you
have gathered a significant number of observations, look over the list for
any ecological patterns - insects that share the same habitat, or the same
seasonality. [Levels: E/I; Subject: science; Skills: analysis/charting
and graphing/identification/listing/observation]

Insect Phenology Calendar. Expand the children's awareness of
seasonal insect activity by keeping a phenology calendar or notebook. The
object is simple: to keep track of the first (or last) dates of insect
activities each year. It's just like keeping an insect diary. Over the
years your notes will provide valuable insight into insect activity in
your local area. Insect activities to record might include the first
sighting of the mourningcloak or monarch butterfly, the first mosquito,
the first chirping cricket, the first singing cicada, the first wasp nest
under construction, the first tent caterpillar webs, the first Junebug, or
the appearance of "snowfleas" (springtails, actually). Perhaps your group
can come up with other insect activities to be looking for! [Levels:
P/E/I; Subject: science; Skills: identification/note keeping/observation]

Aquatic Insect Mini-habitat. Collect a variety of aquatic insects
(and plants) and place them in an aquarium set up to resemble a natural
aquatic habitat. Make notes on the insects' activity. How do they get
air? What do they feed on? How is it that some aquatic insects can walk
on the water, but other terrestrial insects cannot? For more information
on rearing insects see page 25. [Levels: P/E/I; Subject: science; Skills:
critical thinking/keeping notes/observation]

Insect Mini-habitats. Using knowledge about the life history and
habitats of common insects it is possible to set up an indoor mini-habitat
for many types of insects. You can use old aquaria, glass jars, and
plastic sodapop bottles. "Landscape" the container with an appropriate
substrate (gravel, sand, potting soil, etc.) and hiding places (rocks,
wood, or plants). Don't forget a food and moisture supply! Unless you
want to study interactions such as predation and reproduction, it is
generally best to keep different types of insect in separate containers.
Insects that do well for short periods of time in captivity include
antlions, ants, many types of beetles, many types of bugs, caterpillars,
crickets, cockroaches, earwigs, grasshoppers, mantids, stick insects, and
termites. Please release your insects (in the appropriate habitat) after
several weeks. For more information on caring for live insects, see pages
25 and 26 in this book. [Levels: P/E/I; Subject: science; Skills: critical
thinking/decision making/notekeeping/observation/prediction/synthesis]

Bug Autobiography

My name:_____

My size:_____

My shape: _____

My color:_____

My picture!
(draw me or paste a photo)

My habitat (where I live):_____

_____

My season (when I'm active):_____

_____

My favorite foods (what I like to eat):_____

_____

My life cycle (how I grew up):

_____

_____

_____

_____

_____

My "baby" picture
(draw me or paste a photo)

My habits (am I helpful or harmful to people?):

_____

My nearest relatives:_____

My worst enemies:_____

Designed by Gary A. Dunn, Young Entomologists' Society, 1915 Peggy Place, Lansing MI 48910-2553

References: Insect Ecology

About Insects that Help Plants. Gertrude Gibson. Melmont Publishers. Chicago. 1963.

Animals in Disguise. James Poling. W.W. Norton and Co. New York. 1966.

Carnivorous Plants. Nancy Nielson. Franklin Watts. New York. 1992.

Compost Critters. Bianca Lavies. E.P. Dutton. New York. 1993.

From Flower to Flower - Animals and Pollination. Patricia Lauber. Crown Publishers. New York. 1986.

Furtive Fauna. A Guide to the Creatures Who Live on You. Roger M. Knutson. Penguin Books. New York. 1992.

Galls and Gall Insects. Ross Hutchins.

Good Bugs and Bad Bugs in Your Garden - Backyard Ecology. Dorothy Childs Hogner. Thomas Crowell Company. New York. 1974.

How Insects Live. Walter Blaney. Elsevier Press. New York. 1976.

Insect Hibernation. Hidetomo Oda. Raintree Publishers. Milwaukee, WI. 1986.

Insects: Hunters and Trappers. Ross Hutchins. Rand McNally and Co. Skokie, IL. 1957.

Insects and Flowers. Hidetomo Oda. Raintree Publishers. Minneapolis, MN. 1986.

Insects and Plants. Irving and Ruth Adler. John Day and Co. New York. 1962.

Insects and Plants - The Amazing Partnership. Elizabeth Cooper. Harcourt, Brace and World. New York. 1963.

Insects in the Garden. D. M. Souza. Carolrhoda Books. Minneapolis, MN. 1991.

It's a Good Thing There Are Insects! Allan Folwer. Children's Press. Chicago. 1990.

Killer Plants. Mycol Doyle. Lowell House Juvenile. Los Angeles, CA. 1993.

Let's Find Out About Insects. David Knight. Franklin Watts. New York, 1967.

Life on a Little Known Planet. Howard E. Evans. E.P. Dutton and Co. New York. 1968.

The Living Pond. Nigel Hester. Franklin Watts. New York. 1990.

Milkweed Butterfly - Monarchs, Models and Mimics. Hilda Simon. Vaguard Press. New York. 1969.

Our Six-legged Friends and Allies Hilda Simon Vanguard Press. New York. 1971.

Plants and Insects Together. Dorothy Hinshaw Patent. Holiday House. New York. 1976.

Pond Life. Rena Kirkpatrick. Steck-Vaughn Co. Austin, TX. 1991.

Puddles and Ponds. Rose Wyler. Julian Messner. Englewood Cliffs, NJ. 1990.

Where Do Insects Go in Winter? Christine Miskovits. T.S. Dennison. Minneapolis, MN. 1973.

Where Do They Go? Insects in Winter. Millicent E. Selsam. Scholastic, Inc. New York. 1982.

Young Scientist Investigates Pond Life. Terry Jennings. Childrens Press. 1985.

Young Scientist Investigates Small Garden Animals. Terry Jennings. Childrens Press. 1982.

References: Butterfly Gardening

Attracting Butterflies to Eastern Colorado Yard and Garden. Paul A. Opler and Whitney S. Cranshaw. Service in Action Bull. No. 5.504, Colorado State Univ. (1986)

Attracting Insects for Backyard Entomology. Dale Habeck. Florida Entomologist 68(1):117-120 (1984)

Bee Gardening: Wildflowers for Native Bees. Michael Arduser. Wildflower 2(2):6-12 (1989)

Bringing Butterflies to the Garden. Jo Brewer. Horticult. 57:50-9 (1979)

The Butterfly's World. Notes of a Butterfly Gardener. Sharon J. Collman. Univ. Washington Arboretum Bulletin, Summer 1983, 46(:2)

Butterflies Are Free. Maryanne Newsom-Brighton. National Wildlife 20:26-34 (1982)

The Butterfly Book. An Easy Guide to Butterfly Gardening, Identification, and Behavior. Donald and Lillian Stokes and E. Williams. Little, Brown & Co. Boston. 1991.

The Butterfly Garden. Matthew Tekulsky. Harvard Common Press. Cambridge, MA. 1985.

The Butterfly Garden. Creating Gardens to Attract Beautiful Butterflies. Jerry Sedenko. Random House. New York. 1991

Butterfly Gardening. Creating Summer Magic in Your Garden. Xerces Society and Smithsonian Institution. Sierra Club Books. San Francisco, CA. 1990.

Butterfly Gardening for the South. Cultivating Plants that Attract Butterflies. Geyata Ajilvsgi. Taylor Publ. Co. Dallas, TX. 1990.

Butterfly Gardening with Florida's Native Plants. Craig Huegel. Florida Native Plant Society. Orlando, FL. 1992.

Butterfly Gardens Are Soaring. Rachel Snyder. Flower & Garden, Apr. 1989

A Garden of Butterflies. Maryanne Newsom-Brighton. Organic Gardening 30(1):46-48 (1983)

Gardens for Butterflies. Pamela Nelson. Michigan Natural Resources Magazine, March/April 1992.

Grow a Butterfly Garden. Wendy Potter-Springer. Garden Way Publishing. Pownal, VT. 1990.

Handbook for Butterfly Watchers. Robert M. Pyle. Houghton Mifflin. Boston. 1992.

How to Attract Hummingbirds and Butterflies. Ortho Books Staff. Ortho Books. Berkeley, CA. 1991.

Welcome Butterflies. Plantings to Transform Your Yard into a Butterfly Paradise. Douglas A. Jimerson. Better Homes & Gardens, Mar. 1987.

For more information on butterflies, butterfly gardening, and butterfly gardening materials, contact the Young Entomologists' Society (and request a free catalog).

Lesson 8: How Insects and Humans Interact

Key Points

1. Many insects are beneficial to humans because they help people.
   For example:
   - Insects collect or produce useful products such as silk, beeswax, honey, shellac, tannic acid, inks, dyes, and medications.
   - Insects aid in the production of fruits, seeds, vegetables and flowers by pollinating the blossoms.
   - Insects serve as food for many birds and animals. In many parts of the world they are an important source of food for man.
   - Many insects destroy other injurious insects and pests (such as weeds).
   - Insects improve the physical condition of soil and improve its' fertility.
   - Insects are scavengers and eat the bodies of dead animals and plants.

2. A few insects are harmful to humans because they hurt people or destroy property. For example:
   - Insects destroy or damage growing crops and other valuable plants.
   - Insects annoy and injure man and other animals by biting, sucking blood, stinging, spreading disease and living in or on the body.
   - Insects destroy or damage stored products including food, clothing, drugs, animal and plant collections, books, furniture, buildings, wood products and other items.
   - Insects have aesthetic and entertainment value.

3. Insects can be controlled by either applied methods (under the direct control of humans) or natural methods (under the control of nature and not dependent upon humans for success or influence). Applied control methods include (a) chemical controls, (b) physical and mechanical controls (killing insects with machinery or energy), (c) cultural control (killing insects through regular farming practices), (d) biological control (artificial increases in natural enemies) and (e) legal control (creating laws and regulations to prevent the spread of insects). Natural controls include (a) weather (rain, sun, cold, heat and wind), (b) landscape (large lakes, rivers, oceans and mountains), and (c) natural enemies (predators, parasites and pathogens).

4. The best system for controlling pest insects is IPM (integrated pest management). This system uses a combination of many control methods to reduce pest populations to acceptable, affordable levels.

5. Some insect species have changed the course of human history, especially through the spread of disease and famine.

6. Human fascination and amazement with insects has been the origin of many legends, fables, and superstitions. The sacred scarab was worshipped by the Egyptians; many insects (especially ladybird beetles and butterflies) are considered good luck charms. Insects have been the inspiration for designers of airplanes, locomotives, toys, wallpaper, draperies, and much more. Because many of the Aztec designs are similar to patterns found on beetles of that area, the Indians must have borrowed their ideas from the beetles.

7. Because of man's activities and destruction of insect habitat, some insects have become rare, threatened or endangered. Several butterflies and other insects are now extinct. To increase awareness about the importance and value of insects, many states have adopted official state insects.

Activity Ideas

Who's Afraid of the Big Bad Bug? Discuss why people are afraid of insects. Is the fear of insects justified in all cases? How has Hollywood capitalized on people's phobias about insects? Watch and discuss some of the infamous insect fear films, or make a homemade version of your own insect fear film. [Levels: P/E/I; Subject: science/social studies; Skills: communication/creativity/critical thinking]

Shoo, Fly, Don't Bother Me! Here's an activity to challenge your children's problem-solving skills. Have each child list as many ways as they can think of to keep house flies from spreading diseases in your house. After giving the children sufficient time to generate their personal list, create a group list for all to see. [Levels: P/E/I; Subject: science; Skills: critical thinking/invention/problem solving]

Pest Control Then and Now. Have the children ask their parents, grandparents, and great grandparents what methods they used to control insect pests. Check in the library to see if you can find information on how insects might have been controlled in ancient times? Are any of these same methods still used today? Why or why not? [Levels: E/I; Subject: science/social studies; Skills: critical thinking/interview/research]

Insects in the News. Have the children help you gather newspaper articles about insects. These can be kept in a scrapbook or displayed on a bulletin board. You might also want to keep an eye out for the far-fetched stories about insects that appear from time to time in the "checkout stand tabloids". These fictional stories about giant insects (bees, grasshoppers, and even butterflies) can be used to discuss the distinction between science and science fiction. [Levels: P/E/I; Subjects: science/language arts; Skills: critical thinking/reading]

Immigrant Insects. Study the history behind one or more prominent introduced insect pests that are of major concern in your region or state. (Your state agriculture, forestry, and/or natural resources department can provide this type of information.) Show their spread across the country on a map. Was the introduction accidental or deliberate? What can be done to prevent the introduction of pest insects? [Levels: E/I; Subjects; science/social studies; Skills: critical thinking/mapping]

Where Are All the Good Bugs? How many insects, especially beneficial species, are needlessly killed by cars (radiators and windshields) or electric bug zappers? See if the children can design a project to answer this question. [Levels: E/I; Subject; science; Skills: computation/critical thinking/estimating/experimenting/identification]

Incredible Edible Insects. Insects can be more than survival food - they can be delicious! Several types of familiar insects, including crickets, mealworms, super mealworms, waxworms, butterworms, and bee brood, are nutritious and tasty. I would suggest starting with mealworms or waxworms. You can purchase these from a local bait shop or pet store. Insects, like lobsters and crabs, should be cooked while alive (or fresh frozen). Just before you are ready to begin your cooking, separate the insects from any food materials (theirs, not yours) and debris. Also, remove any insects that are not active and healthy looking (light in color) and then wash the remaining insects. Lightly coat a frying pan with cooking spray, oil, or butter and then pre-heat the pan till the oil begins to bubble. Now place the live insects in the pan, stirring occasionally to prevent burning. Remove from the heat when the insects are golden brown. Placing the cooked insects on paper toweling will absorb the excess grease; eat them while they're still warm. Bon appetite! As an extension of this activity, study the possibilities of using insects as human food. Conduct a survey to see what people's acceptance of the idea would be. [Levels: P/E/I; Subjects; science/social studies; Skills: charting/experimenting/interviewing]

Honey Tasting Party. Did you know that honey made from each different kind of nectar has a unique taste? It's true? Try some blind taste tests to see if the children can tell the different types of honey apart. Which do they like best? [Levels: P/E/I; Subjects; science/child development; Skills: charting/decision making/experimenting]

State Insects - Information and/or Nominations. Some states already have officially designated state insects/butterflies (see list below). How about your state? Surrounding states? Information on your state insect (and the state insects of other states) make an interesting bulletin board or showcase. You can easily put together a map of the United States and the appropriate state insects (either as pictures or actual specimens).

OFFICIAL STATE INSECTS/BUTTERFLIES
ALABAMA - monarch butterfly; ARKANSAS - honey bee; California - California dogface butterfly; CONNECTICUT - European praying mantis; DELAWARE - convergent ladybird beetle; GEORGIA - honey bee (insect) and tiger swallowtail (butterfly); FLORIDA - giant swallowtail butterfly (pending); ILLINOIS - monarch butterfly; IOWA - ladybug; KANSAS - viceroy butterfly; LOUISIANA - honey bee; MAINE - honey bee; MARYLAND - Baltimore checkerspot butterfly; MASSACHUSETTS - ladybug; MISSISSIPPI - honey bee (insect) and spicebush swallowtail (butterfly); MISSOURI - honey bee; NEBRASKA - honey bee; NEW HAMPSHIRE - ladybug; NEW JERSEY - honey bee; NEW YORK - nine-spotted ladybird beetle; NORTH CAROLINA - honey bee; OHIO - ladybug (insect) and tiger swallowtail (butterfly/pending); OREGON - Oregon swallowtail butterfly; PENNSYLVANIA - lightningbug; SOUTH CAROLINA - Carolina mantis; SOUTH DAKOTA - honey bee; TENNESSEE - ladybug and firefly; UTAH - honey bee; VERMONT - monarch butterfly; VIRGINIA - tiger swallowtail (butterfly); WISCONSIN - honey bee; and WYOMING - western tiger swallowtail butterfly (pending).

If your state doesn't already have a state insect, why not collect "nominations" from people in your community? You can easily turn this into a group charting exercise by making a large chart to record people's nominations and/or votes on. You might want to start with a couple examples (perhaps your groups favorite candidates) to help people get started. In no time at all you should have a good list of candidates for state insect and some idea of how popular each candidate is! Now its time to learn about the legislative process. What would you have to do to get your nominee designated as the official state insect?

If your state already has an official state insect, why not have the children plan and implement a campaign to nominate an official school, city, or county insect. [Levels: E/I; Subjects: science/social studies; Skills: charting and graphing/communication/interviewing/listing/research]

Save the Bugs! Participate in an insect/butterfly conservation project. Help to improve or create insect habitats. Encourage public officials in your community to conserve insects through resource management (not mowing roadsides and vacant lots, planting wildflowers, etc.). Encourage friends and family to stop swatting every bug they see. Some insects, like mosquitoes will always be pests, but most other insects cause no problem so let them be. [Levels: E/I; Subjects: science/social studies; Skills: application/critical thinking/problem solving/research]

Insect Folklore: Fantasy or Fact? Learn more about insect lore (folktales, legends and superstitions). Have the students share their favorite bit of insect folklore (see references, pages 38 and 39). Is there any scientific explanation or truth to any of these beliefs? Here are some examples:

"When the white butterfly comes, comes also the summer." (Zuni Saying)
"He who would gather the honey must bear the sting of the bees." (Proverb)
"When the gnats swarm, rain and warmer weather are believed to be coming."
    (American Saying)
"Patience and a mulberry leaf become a silk gown." (Chinese Proverb)
"The fatter the flea the leaner the dog." (Proverb)
"Take not a musket to kill a fly." (Proverb)
"When hornets build their nest near the ground a harsh winter is
    expected." (America Folk Saying)
"If the woolybear has a wide band, it will be a mild winter; if it has a
    narrow band it will be a cold winter." (America Folklore)

[Levels: E/I; Subjects: science/social studies; Skills: critical thinking/reading/ research]

A Letter to the Editor. Tell the children that as editor of the local paper they are being asked to write two editorials - one pro and one con - on a controversial insect-related topic. The owner of the paper hasn't decided which stand to take, so both opinions need to be written up just in case. Possible topics include: should the whole community be sprayed with a pesticide to kill a serious insect infestation, should insects be allowed in processed food, should endangered species be protected by law, or should insect collectors have a "hunting" license. Hopefully during the course of this exercise the children will realize that there are two sides to every story, and that two people with the same information on a controversial topic can still disagree. [Levels: E/I; Subjects: science/social studies/language arts; Skills: analysis/ communication/critical thinking/research/synthesis/writing]

Endangered Insects of the United States. Many people, including children, are unaware of the plight of our endangered insects. If your state is home to federal or state-listed rare, threatened, or endangered species (and most are), then this topic is especially important. See if you can identify some of the reasons for insects being endangered. Are the causes direct and/or indirect? Are they caused by humans or natural? Of course being informed is the first step, but you might want to discuss ways that you and the children could help endangered insects. For information on insect conservation, contact the Xerces Society, 10 SW Ash Street, Portland, OR 977204 (phone: 503-222-2788). For information on the rare, threatened, and endangered insects of your state, contact the appropriate Department of Natural Resources, Fish and Game, Wildlife, Conservation, or Environmental Protection.

FEDERAL LIST OF ENDANGERED AND THREATENED INSECTS (as of 9/23/93)
American burying beetle (Nicrophorus americanus): Endangered, e.USA
Delta green ground beetle (Elaphrus viridis): Threatened, CA
Kretschmarr cave mold beetle (Texamaurops reddelli): Endangered, TX
Northeastern beach tiger beetle (Cicidela dorsalis dorsalis): Threatened,
    New England coast
Puritan tiger beetle (Cicindela puritana): Threatened, Connecticut River
Tooth cave ground beetle (Rhadine persephone): Endangered, TX
Valley elderberry longhorn beetle (Desmocerus californicus dimorphus):
    Threatened, CA
Bay checkerspot (Euphydryas editha bayensis): Threatened, CA
El Segundo blue butterfly (Euphilotes battoides allyni): Endangered, CA
Karner blue (Lycaeides melissa samuelis): Endangered, MN/WI/IL/IN/MI/NY/NY
Lange's metalmark butterfly (Apodemia mormo langei): Endangered, west. USA
Lotis blue butterfly (Lycaeides argyrognomon lotis): Endangered, CA)
Mission blue butterfly (Icaricia icaroides missionensis): Endangered, CA
Mitchell's satyr (Neonympha mitchelli mitchelli): Endangered, IN/MI/OH/NJ
Myrtle's silverspot (Speyeria zerene myrtlaea): Endangered, CA
Oregon silverspot (Speyeria zerene hippolyta): Threatened, OR/WA/CA
Palos Verde blue (Glaucopsyche lygdamus palosverdesenis): Endangered, CA
San Bruno elfin (Callophrys mossii bayensis): Endangered, CA
Schaus swallowtail (Heraclides aristodemus ponceanus): Endangered, FL
Smith's blue butterfly (Euphilotes enoptes smithi): Endangered, CA
Uncompahgre fritillary (Boloria acrocnema): Endangered, CO
Kern primrose sphinx moth (Euproserpinus euterpe): Threatened, CA
Ash Meadows creeping water bug (Ambrysus amargosus): Threatened, NV
Pawnee montane skipper (Hesperia leonard montana): Threatened, CO
Delhi sands flower-loving fly (Rhaphiomidas terminatus abdominalis):
    Endangered, CA

Non-native insects listed by the U.S. Fish and Wildlife Service:
Luzon peacock swallowtail (Papilio chikae): Endangered, Philippines
Homerus swallowtail (Papilio homerus): Endangered, Jamaica
Corsican swallowtail (Papilio hospiton): Endangered, Corsica (France)
Queen Alexandra birdwing (Troides alexandrae): Endangered, New Guinea

Complete information on the 700 endangered and threatened plants and animals listed by the U.S. Fish and Wildlife Service is now available on CD-ROM. These disks contain detailed information such as status reports, recovery plans, and more. Contact Fas-Track Computer Products (7030C Huntley Road, Columbus, OH 43229-1053, tel. 1-800-927-3936) or TigerSoftware (One Datran Center, 9100 S. Dadeland Blvd Suite 1500, Miami, FL 33156, tel. 1-800-238-4437).

References

Battle on the Rosebush. Marian Edsall. Follett Publishing Co. Chicago. 1972.

Bee: Friend of Flowers. Paul Starosta. Charlesbridge Publishers. Cambridge, MA. 1991.

But Will It Bite Me? Edith Bailes. Cardamon Press. Richmond, ME. 1984.

Cleaning Nature Naturally. Kathlyn Gay. Walker and Co. New York. 1991.

Cockroaches. Joanna Cole. William Morrow and Co. New York. 1971.

Disaster! Insect Attack. Christopher Lampton. Millbrook Press. Brookfield, CT. 1992.

Friendly Bees. Ferocious Bees. Mona Kerby. Franklin Watts. New York. 1987.

Insect Pests. George Fichter and Howard Zim. Golden Press. New York. 1966.

Killer Bees. Laurence Pringle. Morrow Junior Books. New York. 1990.

Should Bugs Bug You? Beau Fly Jones. Zaner-Bloser. Columbus, OH. 1990.

Silkworms. Sylvia Johnson. Lerner Publications. Minneapolis, MN. 1982.

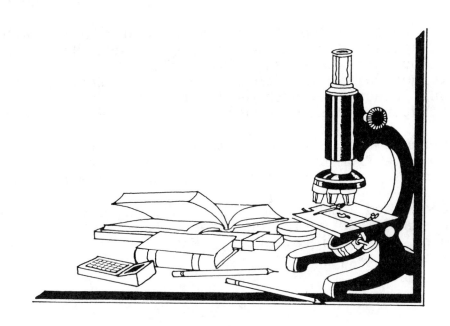

Lesson 9: Participation in the Entomological Community

Many opportunities, including career exploration, exist for young people interested in entomology.

Key Points

1. Various clubs and organizations, like the Young Entomologists Society, exist for youths, amateurs, and professionals interested in entomology. These organizations allow members to share their knowledge and expertise about insects with one another. (See the "Insect Study Sourcebook" for a list of entomological societies in the United States and other countries.)

2. Insects can be "collected" from other states, regions, or countries by exchanging or trading with someone in the desired area.

3. There are many exciting careers in entomological sciences.

Activity Ideas

An After School or Neighborhood Bug Club. Help interested children set up an after school or Saturday bug club. Suggestions for club organization, activities, resources, and leadership is available from the Young Entomologists' Society.

Join the Young Entomologists' Society. Encourage interested children to join the Young Entomologists Society, an international bug club for kids and adults. Call or write for enrollment forms. They will receive low-cost publications, help from Society staff and members, and an opportunity to have their drawings and stories published by the Society.

Interview An Entomologist. Invite a member of a nearby entomological society, entomology or biology department, beekeeper, or pest control operator to speak to your class about the field of entomology or about his/her particular job or specialty. Have the children prepare a few questions in advance, such as "What do you do for your work"?, "How did you get interested in entomology?", and "What's your favorite insect"?

The Big Bug Swap. Set up a specimen or information exchange program with young people from other schools and/or countries. Assistance for making contacts is available from the Young Entomologists' Society.

Buggy Books and Information. Have the children help build a library of literature and information on insects (newspaper and magazine articles, picture books, field guides, etc.). Make the library readily available to all interested children.

References
(See page 40 also)

A Beginner's Guide to Observing and Collecting Insects. Gary A. Dunn. Young Entomologists' Society. Lansing, MI. 1994. (Career and scholarship information.)
A Day in the Life of a Beekeeper. Penny Michels and Judith Tropea. Troll Associates. Mahwah, NJ. 1991.
The Insect Study Sourcebook. Gary A. Dunn. Young Entomologists;' Society. Lansing, MI. 1994.

FINAL WRAP UP

Evaluation is an important step in the learning process. It provides a review of knowledge and skills learned. The evaluation process also allows you to see how the children have applied what they learned. You may want to use one of the following activities as a way for evaluating the childrens' grasp of the knowledge presented in your insect unit (especially where grading is not appropriate or necessary).

Have Bugs, Will travel. Arrange for a visit by the Y.E.S. "Bugs-On-Wheels" program staff (write or call the Young Entomologists' Society for a FREE brochure). Other outreach programs and bugmobiles are also listed in "The Insect Study Sourcebook" by Gary A. Dunn (Young Entomologists' Society. Lansing, MI. 1994.)

Fair Time. Have an "insect fair" to exhibit all of the insect projects, crafts, displays, drawings, experiments, models, and/or collections. Exhibiting completed projects at the school, local community center, public library, shopping mall, or other public place provides recognition to the children and also help increase public awareness about the importance of insects. The children can perform insect skits, songs, stories, or demonstrations to help share insect information with other children, teachers, administrators, and parents. You can even serve special "buggy" refreshments such as those mentioned on page 9). Additional suggestion can be found in "Organizing Bug Days and Insect Fairs" by Gary A. Dunn (Young Entomologists' Society. Lansing, MI. 1994.)

Your Children As Published Authors. The Young Entomologists' Society is unique in its regular use of youth submitted materials in its periodical publications. You are strongly encouraged to submit original stories, poems, informative articles, and artwork for possible publication in "Insect World" or "Y.E.S. Quarterly". Those materials that are chosen will be read by thousands of bug enthusiasts around the world!

Off to the Bug Races. Here's another fun way to evaluate how much everybody has learned. This game can be played on a large game board, or on an overhead projector. You will need a racetrack with 15 to 25 mileposts (on cardboard or overhead transparency), velcro (board version only), small cutout of insects (or small rubber bugs), and index cards with questions (once again the Smithsonian Insect Quiz or .... are a good source of questions). Divide the children into teams (its better to have smaller teams and a larger number of race lanes). Playing is simple: each question answered correctly moves the insect ahead one milepost. Incorrect answers neither penalize nor advance an insect. If the question is answered incorrectly by a team, pass it on to the next team. If the question remains unanswered or correctly answered, continue until each team has had a shot at it. If no one answers correctly, discuss the correct answer with the class. Poor sportsmanship or calling out answers can cause an insect to stumble and lose ground (to be determined by the teacher). The first insect to cross the finish line wins. The game can be continued to see who takes second and third place.

Insect Name Calling - Again! Ask the children to name all the insects they can think of. Get out the list(s) that the children made at the beginning of the unit. It's a sure bet that the list at the end of the unit will be at least two or three times longer than the list you made on the first day! Or, if you used an insect facts quiz, have the children do it again to see how much they have improved.

Test Your Insect Knowledge. Why not challenge the children and test their knowledge on the fascinating world of insects with a skill contest. This can be done interactively, or as self-study. You can test general insect knowledge using questions, and insect identification using pictures. A good source of questions is the Smithsonian Insect Quiz (available from the Young Entomologists' Society or other science suppliers) and "Organizing Bug Days and Insects Fairs" by Gary A. Dunn (Young Entomologists' Society. Lansing, MI, 1994.) Or, ask the children to help with generating questions for use.

The <u>Wheel</u> of <u>Wonder</u>. A roulette wheel can be easily constructed and divided into 16 or more sections; label each section with a letter or number. A series of questions or pictures (insects to be identified) can be set up on a separate board. The Smithsonian Insect Quiz or other source of trivia can be used to generate some challenging questions. Insect Cards (like those available from Y.E.S.) are a good source of illustrations (with the names blocked out). Have a contestant spin the wheel; when the wheel stops spinning they must answer the question or identify the insect that corresponds to the letter or number on the wheel. Prizes for correct answers can be given (but are not necessary).

The <u>Insect</u> <u>Quiz</u> <u>Board</u>. A quiz board is relatively simple to construct. Start with a 2 foot square piece of plywood. Sand the board until it is smooth. Arrange insect pictures (or questions) on the board and glue in place. If cut-out names (answers) are being used, apply them now, too. (Hint: If you would like to change the pictures/questions periodically, glue plastic card holders in place instead.) Apply a coat of varnish or clear polyeurethane over the board and pictures; this helps seal them to the board. The board should be sanded lightly with very fine sandpaper between each coat. Several coats may be needed, depending on the degree of gloss desired. When the last coat of finish is dry, attach the board to the frame. Drill holes for the bolts under each picture (question) and under each name (answer). To save money, use two pronged brass paper fasteners as contacts instead of the more expensive carriage bolts. To avoid confusion and mistakes in wiring, it is best to insert only two bolts at a time, one under the picture (question) the other under the proper name (answer). Wire these two bolts together before moving on to the next pair. Attach the wires to the bolts as shown in the side view illustration below. Be sure to peel off enough of the coating from the wire to assure that the bare wire is in good contact with the metal of the bolt. After all the wires are connected it's time to attach the battery and light/socket. One wire should go from one of the battery terminals to the top of the front panel, and through a hole in the front of the board. Another wire goes from the other battery terminal to the base of the bulb socket. Another piece of wire goes from the other socket terminal through a hole in the front of the board (see the diagram). Attach a nail, bolt, or alligator clip to the end of each wire and the quiz board is ready for use. Another piece of plywood, or a piece of cardboard, can be attached to the back of the quizboard to protect the wiring. This should be put on with only a few screws so that it can be removed easily to replace the battery as needed.

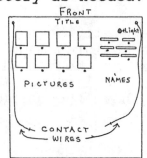

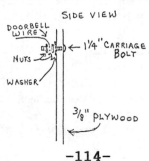

Insect Jeopardy. The format of this well-known television game show can be used to test insect knowledge. The object of the game is to provide the correct question to an answer displayed on the board. To play the game you must construct a special game board. The game board should be constructed out of a 4x8' sheet of plywood covered with fabric (any type that velcro will stick to) or nicely painted. Across the top put the words "BUG JEOPARDY". On the remainder of the board you will need room for 4 to 6 columns (different topics) and 5 rows (the questions). The topic names and questions can be fastened using any of several different methods. The cards can simply be hung from eye hooks; they can be attached with velcro and clips; or, plastic sleeves can be glued or velcroed in place and the cards slipped into the sleeves. After the board is constructed you will need to generate a large supply of answers (to which the players will provide the questions). For example, the answer in the category "Insect Orders" might be "characterized by scaly wings and coiled proboscis"; the appropriate question would be "what is the order Lepidoptera". The 10 point questions should be easier than the 50 point questions.

One player is chosen to go first (by coin toss) and picks a category and answer. The question is revealed, and the player attempts to provide the correct question. Another player may beat him/her to the punch by signaling first. If the question is correctly given the appropriate number of points are awarded to the winning player; if an incorrect question is given the points are deducted from the score and the other players are given an opportunity to supply the correct question. Play until all of the answers on the board have been revealed.

Insect Quiz Bowl. This form of competition predates "Jeopardy", and uses the more traditional question, then answer, format. This game generally does not require an elaborate game board, but special electronic buzzers and lights are often used to separate the split second reaction times of contestants. One source of electronic quiz bowl equipment is NASCO (P.O. Box 901, Fort Atkinson, WI 53538-0901). This game is generally played by teams, but could be played by individuals as well.

First, a "toss-up" question is read aloud and the teams (or individuals) attempt to be the first to buzz in and supply the correct answer. If the question is correctly answered they get a point (and a followup bonus question); if answered incorrectly the opposing team gets an opportunity to answer the question (and a bonus question if answered correctly).

Improvisational Bug Play. Divide the children into small groups, and give each group a box of "props". The "prop" box should include an assortment of any of the following items: newspaper, paper plates, styrofoam shapes, straws, paper towel rolls, balloons, string or yarn, egg cartons, buttons, paper bags, tongue depressors, chenilles, scraps of construction paper, and any other "arts-and-crafty" items you can come up with. Each group should also be supplied with masking tape, white glue, a stapler, and scissors. Inform each group that they have 20 minutes to turn the items in their box into props for a "buggy play (skit)", which they will perform for the rest of group. Their skit should tell a story about the habits, behavior, or life cycle of an insect. [Level: E/I; Subjects: science/arts; Skills: communication/ synthesis/creativity/ cooperation/decision making/invention/public speaking/small group work]

Insect Scavenger Hunt. The traditional scavenger hunt can still be used as a fun way to check a groups insect knowledge. Prepare a list of items to be collected. Divide the group into teams and give each copies of the list. Each team can also be assigned a collection box, a place to accumulate their items until you have time to check them off.

Suggested items might include:
> A picture of an insectivorous plant.
> The shed exoskeleton of an insect.
> An insect-produced plant gall.
> A specimen of a larval Lepidoptera. (Release when done.)
> An insect with one pair of wings.
> The name of the world's smallest insect. (Fairyfly)
> A model of an insect.
> A diagram showing the major parts of an insect's body.
> The name of a famous entomologist.
> A piece of wood with insect tunnels in it.
> An insect egg.
> A list of ten common butterflies and beetles.
> A rubber or plastic insect replica.
> A leaf partially eaten by an insect.
> Any insect with sucking mouthparts.
> Name of the world's biggest butterfly (Queen Alexandra birdwing)
> A book with poems about insects.
> An insect that lives in the water.
> A product made by insects and used by humans.
> An insect pupa.
> Any insect exhibiting gradual metamorphosis.
> A brochure on controlling insect pests.
> The name of a common insect in another language.
> The name and location of a famous insect museum.

Buggy Awards and Incentives. Don't underestimate the importance of giving lots of verbal praise for all childrens' accomplishments. For those special occasions where a prize or incentive award is appropriate, a variety of inexpensive items (patches, buttons, pencils, rubber bugs, stickers, etc.) are available from the Young Entomologists' Society and other suppliers.

Bug Nut Trophy. Children can make their own Bug Nut Trophies, or you can make them as awards and incentives. You will need a small wood block, 2-3" square (best cut from a long piece of baseboard molding), a walnut, and a small rubber bug. On the tapered edge of the molding write the words "Bug Nut" with a marker or paint. Decorate the walnut with eyes, nose, and mouth. Small doll eyes and doll hats can also be glued on for special looks (these are available at many craft stores). Glue the walnut and small rubber bug next to each other on the molding, with the bug on the left and the walnut on the right.

References

The Insect Study Sourcebook. Gary A. Dunn Young Entomologists'
    Society. Lansing, MI. 1994.
Organizing Bug Days and Insect Fairs. Gary A. Dunn. Young
    Entomologists' Society. Lansing, MI. 1994.

GLOSSARY OF ENTOMOLOGICAL WORDS

Aestivation [ess-ti-VAY-shun] A special tyope of dormancy during a warm
   or dry season which allows insects to survive during periods of
   extreme heat and/or drought.
Amber [am-BURR] Fossilized tree sap, often containing insects.
Antenna [ann-TEN-ah] A pair of jointed appendages located on the head
   of an insect above the mouthparts, which are used for feeling
   (touching), smelling, and hearing.
Arachnid [ah-RACK-nid] A type of small animal characterized by a hard
   external skeleton, two body sections, eight legs, fang-like pincers
   and simple eyes. Common examples of arachnids include spiders, ticks,
   and mites.
Arborial [are-BOR-ee-al] Living on trees and other large plants.
Aspirator [asp-PER-ray-tor] A simple suction devicefor picking up
   small insects.
Aquatic [ah-KWA-tic] Living in the water, at least for most of the life
   cycle.
Arthropod [ARE-throw-pod] The largest group of animals, characterized
   by an exoskeleton and jointed body parts. Includes animals such as
   spiders, scorpions, horseshore crabs, crustaceans, millipedes,
   centipedes, and insects.

Beak [beek] The long, pointed mouth structures of an insect with
   piercing-sucking mouthparts, such as true bugs (Hemiptera) and the
   cicadas and relatives (Homoptera).
Berlese funnel [burr-LAY-see FUN-nel] An insect collecting device that
   consists of a large funnel containing a piece of screen, with a
   container below it; materials, such as leaf litter, soil, or rotting
   wood, is placed in the funnel and heat from a light placed above the
   funnel forces the hidden insects down the funnel into the container.
Brood [BREWED] All of the individual insects that hatch from the eggs
   laid by one mother, or individuals that hatch at about the same time
   and normally mature at about the same time.

Camouflage [kam-OH-floj] The use of color patterns, shape, and/or
   behavior to remain concealed from predators or prey.
Carnivorous [car-NIV-or-us] feeding on the flesh of other animals.
Caste [KAST] a form or type of adult in a social insect colony, such as
   a soldier or worker.
Caterpillar [KAT-er-pill-er] A special type of insect larvae with a
   cylindrical body, distinct head capsule, chewing mouthparts, thoiracic
   legs, abdominal prolegs; the common name for the larval stage of a
   butterfly, moth, swafly or scorpionfly.
Caudal [caw-DULL) Referring to the tail or rear part of an insect's
   body, for example caudal filaments.
Cell [sell] An area in the membrane of an insect wing that is partly
   (open cell) or completely (closed cell) surrounded by veins.
Cercus [cer-SUS] A short, feeler-like appendage located on an insect's
   abdomen, near the tip.
Chelicera [chay-LISS-era] The fang-like mouthparts of arachnids
   (spiders, scorpions, and mites).
Chitin [KITE-in] a special chemical compound (nitrogenous
   polysaccharide) occuring in the skeleton of insects that is
   responsible for the resilence of the body wall.
Chrysalis [KRISS-ah-liss] The pupa of a butterfly.
Clubbed antenna [KLUBD ann-TEN-nah] The outer antennal segments are
   expanded, enlarged, or swollen and resemble a club.

Cocoon [KAH-coon] A silken case in which the pupa is formed. Common in moths and some beetles.

Complete metamorphosis [kum-PLEAT met-ah-MORE-fuh-sis] A complex type of insect development with four distinct stages - egg, larva, pupa and adult.

Compound eye [kom-POUND I] The major insect eye, composed of many individual facets or lenses

Cornicle [kor-NICKLE] One of a pair of tubular structures extending from the posterior part of an aphid's abdomen.

Crawler [KRAWL-er] The active first immature of a scale insect.

Crochets [kro-SHAYS] The hooked spines at the tip of the prolegs of caterpillars.

Cuticle [Q-tickle] The noncellular outer layer of the body wall of an arthropod. (See also chitin.)

Diapause [DIE-ah-paws] A period of arrested development.

Dichotomous key [die-KOT-ah-muss KEE] An identification tool that uses paired statements to assist a person in learning the identity of an insect (or other organism).

Diurnal [die-UR-nal] Active during the daylight hours.

Drone The male bee.

Ectoparasite [ek-toe-PAIR-ah-site] A parasite that lives and feeds on the outside of its host.

Elytron [ee-LYE-tron] A thickened, armor-like forewing, found in the beetles and weevils (Coleoptera) and earwigs (Dermaptera).

Emergence [ee-MERJ-ants] The act of an adult insect leaving the pupal case or the last immature 4exoskeleton.

Entomologist [en-toe-MOL-oh-jist] A person who studies the life cycles, behavior, ecology, or diversity of insects as their work or hobby.

Entomology [en-toe-MOL-oh-gee] The study of insects, their life cycles, behavior, ecology, diversity and control.

Exoskeleton [ex-o-SKEL-ah-ton] The skelton or supporting structure on the outside of an arthropod's body.

Femur [fee-MUR] The third leg segment, located just above the tibia

Fossorial [foss-ORE-ee-al] Equipped with special body parts for digging in the soil.

Frass [FRAS] Plant fragments made by plant-feeding insects, usually mixed with excrement.

Gall [GAWL] An abnormal growth (tumor) of plant tissues caused by the stimulus of an insects, bacteria, or another plant.

Gradual metamorphosis [grad-U-awl met-ah-MORE-fuh-sis] A relatively simple type of insect development with three distinct stages - egg, nymph, and adult.

Gregarious [greh-GARE-ee-us] Living in groups.

Halter [hal-TUR] A small knob-like balancing organ located in place of the hindwing in the true flies (Diptera)

Head [hed] The frontal body region; the section which bears the antennae, eyes, and mouthparts.

Herbivorous [her-BIV-or-us] Feeding on plants.

Hibernation hye-bur-nay-SHUN] Dormancy during the winter.

Hive [hyv] The home of a bee colony.

Honeydew [hun-ee do] A liquid discharged by certain insects (aphids, scales, mealybugs) that is high in sugar content.

Host The organism in or on which a parasite lives; the plant on which an insect feeds.
Humerus [HEW-mur-us] The shoulder of an insect, formed by the forward angle of the front wings.

Imago [im-MAH-go] The adult or reproductive stage of an insect.
Incomplete metamorphosis [in-kum-PLEAT met-ah-MORE-fuh-sis] A moderately complex type of insect development with three distinct stages - egg, naiad, and adult.
Insect [IN-sekt] A type of small animal characterized by a hard external skeleton, three body sections, six legs, single pair of antennae, wings, and compound eyes. Common examples of insects include grasshoppers, true bugs, beetles, butterflies, moths, true flies, ants, bees and wasps.
Insectivorus [in-sek-TIV-or-us] Feeding on inscets.
Instar [in-STAR] The stage of an insects between successive molts; the first instar is the stage between hatching and the first molt.

Joint [joynt] A flexible area that permit movement of two adjoining body paryts or appendages.

Larva [lar-VAH] The immature stage, between the egg and the pupa, of an insect having complete metamorphosis. (See also complete metamorphosis.)
Leaf miner [leef mine-ur] An insect that lives and feeds on the leaf cells between the upper and lower surfaces of the leaf.
Life cycle The sequence of all developmental events that occur from birth (egg hatch) to reproduction (mating and egg laying).
Looper [lew-PURR] A caterpillar that moves by looping its body, that is, placing the posterior part of the abdomen next to the thorax and then extending the front part of the body forward. Also known as a measuringworm or inchworm.

Maggot [mah-GUT] The legless larva without a well-developed head capsule; the larva of a fly.
Mandibles The paired, pincer-like jaws of an insect with chewing mouthparts, such as grasshoppers, cockroaches, beetles and ants.
Membranous wings Insect wings made of a thin film of tissue that is usually transparent.
Metamophosis [met-ah-MORE-fuh-sis] Change in form during development.
Mimicry [mim-eh-KREE] The ability of an insect to imitate or mimic another species of animal or plant in form and color, sometimes behavior as well.
Molt The process of shedding the exoskeleton.
Moniliform [mahn-nil-EE-form] Beadlike, with rounded segments (antenna).
Mouthparts [MOWTH-parts] The collection of body appendages used by insects to take in food.

Naiad [NYE-add] An aquatic, gill-breathing immature insect. (See also incomplete metamorphosis.)
Nectar [nek-TAR] A sugary liquid produced by flowers to help attract insect pollinators.
Nocturnal [knock-TUR-noll] Active at night.
Nymph [nimf] An immature wingless stage (following hatching) that does not have a pupal stage. (See also gradual metamorphosis.)

Ocellus [oh-SELL-us] A simple eye of an insect or other arthropod
Ommatidium [oh-ma-TID-eum] A single unit or visual section of a
  compound eye.
Ootheca [oh-oh-THEE-kah] The covering or case of an egg mass.
Ova [OH-vah] An insect egg.
Ovipositor [oh-vee-POS-i-tor] The elongate structure located at the
  tip of a female insect's abdomen that helps her lay the eggs. The
  ovipositor may be especially designed for putting eggs into wood,
  soil, or other animals. Some insects (like bees and wasps) may have
  the ovipositor modified into a stinger.

Palp [palp] A segmented extension, fingerlike in shape, associated with
  the mouthparts.
Parasite [pair-AH-site] An animal that lives on or in the body of
  another animal (its host), and which usually does not kill its host or
  consume a large proportion of its tissue.
Pectinate [PEK-tin-ate] With branches or projections like the teeth of
  a comb. (antenna)
Petiole [pet-EE-ole] The stalk or stem by which the abdomen is attached
  to the thorax, most commonly seen in some wasps and ants.
Pheromone [fair-ah-moan] An external substance given off by an insect
  which casuses a specific reaction by other members of the same
  species; includes trail making pheromeones, sex attractants, and alarm
  substances.
Phytophagous [fye-TOF-ah-gus] Feeding on plants.
Plumose [plew-MOOHS] Feather-like, usually referring to antennae,
  palps, or body hairs.
Predator [pred-AH-tor] An animal that attacks and feeds on other
animals (its prey), usually animals smaller and less powerful than itself.
Prey [pray] The food animals of a predator.
Proboscis [pro-BOSS-iss] The extended, coiled mouthparts of
  butterflies and moths, and some other insects.
Proleg [PRO-leg] One of the unjointed, fleshy abdominal legs of certain
  insect larvae, most noteably caterpillars and sawflies.
Pronotum [pro-NO-tum] The dorsal body plate of the thorax, frequently
  enlarged and prolonged in many insects.
Prothorax [pro-THOR-axe] The forwardmost of the three thoracic
  segments.
Pubescent [pew-BESs-ent] Covered with short, downy hairs.

Queen [Kween] The primary reproductive female in a colony of social
  insects (bees, wasps or termites).

Raptorial [rap-TOR-ee-all] Insect legs that are especially fitted for
  grasping prey.
Reproductives [Wree-pro-DUCK-tivs] The members of a social insect
  colony, male and female, that are capable of reproducing; the males
  are referred to as either drones (bees and wasps) or kings (termites)
  and the females are referred to as queens.

Scavenger [SKAV-en-jer] An animal that feeds on the remains of dead
  plants and animals.
Scutellum [skew-TELL-um] A segment of the pronotum, appearing as a more
  or less triangular segment behind the pronotum, most noticable in the
  true bugs (Hemiptera), cicadas and relatives (Homoptera) and the
  beetles (Coleoptera)
Segment A subdivision of the body or of an appendage, between joints
  (sutures).

Serrate [CER-rate] With a saw-like edge, usually on the antennae, claws or sides of the body.

Seta [see-TAH] An external bristle.

Solitary [sol-EH-tarry] Living along, and not in groups.

Spine A sharp, thornlike outgrowth of the exoskeleton.

Spinneret [SPIN-erh-ret] A structure with which silk is spun, usually fingerlike in shape.

Spiracle [SPEAR-ah-kuhl] An external opening of the tracheal respiratory system; a breathing pore

Spittle [spit-uhl] A protective, waterlike substance produced by the immatures of the spittlebugs (froghoppers)

Stigma [STIG-mah] A thickening of the wing membrane along the front edge of the wing near the tip.

Suture [sue-CHUR] An external line-like groove in the exoskeleton, or a narrow membranous area between segments.

Tarsal claw [tar-SULL klaw] One of a pair of claws located near the tip of the last tarsal segment.

Tarsus [tar-SUS] The leg segment beyond the tibia, composed of 3 to 5 small segments.

Tegmen [teg-MEN] The thickened, leathery forewing of a grasshopper, cricket, mantid, or cockroach.

Terrestrial [tare-RES-tree-ahl] Living on land.

Thorax [THOR-axe] The body region behind the head, which bears the legs and wings (when present).

Tibia [TIB-ee-ah] The fourth segment of the leg, located between the femur and tarsus; usually long and slender.

Trachea [TRAK-ee-ah] A tube of the resopiratory systrem, ending externally at the spiracle and terminating internally at the tracheoles.

Tracheoles [TRAK-ee-ols] The fine terminal branches of the respiratory tubes.

Tympanum [tim-PAN-umm] A membrane that is capable of vibrating (for sound production) or use as an auditory organ (eardrum).

Vein [vane] A thickened line which provides supprot in the wing of an insect.

Vertex [VIR-tex] The top of the head

Vestigial [ves-TIJ-all] A body part that is small, poorly developed, and/or non-functional.

Warning colors A pattern of bright colors intended to help other animals avoid a creature because it is poisonous or venomous.

Worker [WHUR-kur] The members of a social insect colony, usually female, that have responsibility for nest maintenance, food gathering, and care of the brood.

APPENDIX: INSECT STUDY RESOURCES

YOUNG ENTOMOLOGISTS' SOCIETY

INSECT WORLD - Our bimonthly bugletter for kids and families interested
    in insects. Each issue contains a special activity and/or coloring
    sheet.
FLEA MARKET - our bimonthly newsletter of classified advertisements by
    people looking to buy, sell or trade insects (dead and alive),
    equipment, books, and much more.
Y.E.S. QUARTERLY - our quarterly journal of international amateur
    entomology.
SPECIAL PUBLICATIONS SERIES - a series of helpful handbooks on many
    aspects of entomological study (finding resources, teaching methods,
    insect identification, rearing, and collecting).
Y.E.S. "BUGGY BOOKSTORE" - the Society carries nearly 600 educational
    materials on insects, spiders, earthworms, and snails, including
    books, kits, study equipment, puppets, rubber "bugs", audiovisuals,
    posters, puzzles, stencils, rubber stamps, stickers, pencils,
    bookmarks, gift items, buttons, hats, and T-shirts. For information
    on current availability and prices of these items contact the Young
    Entomologists' Society, Inc., Dept. PB, 1915 Peggy Place, Lansing MI
    48910-2553, tel. (517) 887-0499, and request a FREE catalog.

BUGS-ON-WHEELS - give your young people a chance to explore the
    fascinating world of insects right in your own community. Live
    insects, vivid pictures, bizarre and beautiful insect specimens (from
    near and far), unique props, exciting activities, and an entertaining
    presentation will enhance your curriculum and involve your whole group
    in an experience they will remember for a long time to come. For more
    information, including current rates and scheduling information,
    contact the Young Entomologists' Society (1915 Peggy Place, Lansing,
    MI 48910-2553), or phone (517) 887-0499.

SOURCES OF INSECT AUDIO-VISUALS

Films and Videos:
    Carolina Biological Supply Co., 2700 York Road, Burlington NC 27215
    Educational Images, P.O. Box 3456 West Side, Elmira NY 14905
    Films Inc. Video, 5547 Ravenswood Ave., Chicago IL 60640-1199
    International Film Bureau, 332 S. Michigan Ave., Chicago IL 60604
    Modern Talking Pictures, 5000 Park Street N., St. Petersburg FL 33709
    Schoolmasters Science, P.O. Box 1941, Ann Arbor MI 48106
    Young Entomologists' Society, 1915 Peggy Place, Lansing, MI 48910-2553
(Note: Check your local video store or public library for documentaries
such as "Life on Earth", "The Helstrom Chronicles", and other
nature/wildlife series with insect titles.)

Overhead Transparencies:
    Carolina Biological Supply Co. (see address above)
    Hubbard/Jewel, P.O. Box 104, Northbrook IL 60065
    Milliken/TIMCO, 14965 Riverside Dr., Livonia MI 48154

35mm Slides:
    Carolina Biological Supply Co. (see address above)
    Eagle River Media, 13401 Bragaw Street, Anchorage AK 99516
    Scavengers, P.O. Box 211328, Auke Bay AK 99821
    Wards Natural Science, P.O. Box 92912, Rochester NY 14623

Educational Software:
    Carolina Biological Supply Co. (see address on previous page)
    Connecticut Valley Biological, P.O. Box 326, Southampton MA 01073
    Diversified Educational, 725 Main St., Lafayette IN 47901
    Drenkow Media, 10306 E. Live Oak Ave., Arcadia CA 91007
    Entomation, 2742 Beacon Hill, Ann Arbor MI 48104
    Fas-Track Computer Products, 7030C Huntley Road, Columbus OH 43229
    Knowledge Adventure, 4502 Dyer Street, La Crescenta CA 91214
    Maxis, 2 Theatre Square Suite 230, Orinda CA 94563-3041
    Wieser Educational, 3005 Comercio, Rancho Santa Margarita CA 92688

MUSEUMS AND INSECT COLLECTIONS

Many colleges and universities, nature centers, science centers, and
natural history museums have insect collections. Call or write to make
arrangements before visiting the collection. Most curators would be very
happy to show you "their" collection if you give them time to prepare for
your visit. A list of museums with insect collections and displays can be
found in "The Insect Study Sourcebook" by Gary A. Dunn (available from the
Young Entomologists' Society).

INSECT ZOOS AND BUTTERFLY HOUSES

Insect zoos and butterfly houses make an excellent field trip site to see
live insects. A complete list of the insect zoos and butterfly houses of
North America (and the rest of world) can be found in "The Insect Study
Sourcebook" by Gary A. Dunn, which is available from Y.E.S.

SOURCES OF COLLECTING EQUIPMENT AND SUPPLIES+

BioQuip Products, Inc., 17803 LaSalle Ave., Gardena CA 90248
Carolina Biological Supply Co., 2700 York Road, Burlington NC 27215
Young Entomologists' Society, 1915 Peggy Place, Lansing MI 48910-2553

SOURCES OF LIVING ARTHROPODS*

Insect Livestock:
    Carolina Biological Supply Co., 2700 York Road, Burlington NC 27215
    Rainbow Mealworms, 126 East Spruce St., Compton CA 90220
    Wards Natural Science, P.O. Box 92912, Rochester NY 14692-9012

Life Cycle and Culture Kits:
    Carolina Biological Supply Co. (address above)
    Papillon Distributors, P.O. Box 1463, Waltham MA 02254
    Young Entomologists' Society (address above)

* For the world's most complete list of livestock suppliers, refer to
"The Insect Study Sourcebook" by Gary A. Dunn (available from the Y.E.S.).

YOUNG ENTOMOLOGISTS' SOCIETY, INC.
SPECIAL PUBLICATION SERIES

THE INSECT STUDY SOURCEBOOK: AN INTERNATIONAL ENTOMOLOGY RESOURCE GUIDE
A complete guide to more than 1200 individuals, businesses, and organizations around the world that can provide insect study products and services - just about everything you need from A to Z! Includes world's most complete list of insect zoos, butterfly houses, and entomological organizations. A must for insect enthusiasts and teachers. Softcover, 128pp.

BUGGY BOOKS: A GUIDE TO JUVENILE AND POPULAR BOOKS ON INSECTS AND THEIR RELATIVES. This annotated directory presents complete details (including quality ratings) on 736 "bug" books for children and educators (cross-referenced by subject matter, reading level, and authors). Locate the good books and avoid the bad ones! 120pp.

BUG CLUB LEADER GUIDE. A complete guide to starting and running your own local bug club. Includes tips for working with young people, teaching techniques, meeting and activity suggestions, and an insect study resource list. 18pp.

THE INSECT IDENTIFICATION GUIDE. This guide makes learning insect identification easy! Includes basic classification and identification methods, basic insect biology, key recognition features for important insect orders and families, diagrammatic and word keys to important insect orders and families (including aquatic insects and immatures), cross-referenced lists to insect common and scientific names, and resource materials. Softcover, 72pp.

THE CASE FOR LIVE PUBLIC BUTTERFLY HABITATS IN THE UNITED STATES. If you want know more about the inner workings of butterfly houses in the USA, then this publication is for you. Features information on live butterfly "habitats", how live butterfly environments can serve the public, experiences of existing exhibits, specific components of live butterfly environment, and developing live butterfly environments. 33pp.

CARING FOR INSECT LIVESTOCK: AN INSECT REARING MANUAL. This manual provides complete information and "tips" for rearing 60 different insects and arthropods. Features the advice of 43 rearing experts that has been compiled and edited into a single treatise. Anyone who raises live insects and other arthropods, for whatever reason, will find this handbook invaluable. Softcover, 96pp.

ORGANIZING BUG DAYS AND INSECT FAIRS. This manual discusses many topics of importance to the organizer of a "bug day" or "insect fair" at parks, nature centers, and museums, or an insect theme day at schools and daycare centers, from initial planning to followup after the event. Features hundreds of tips, resource ideas, and activity suggestions, as well as dozens of ready-to-use reproducible handouts and an extensive bibliography. Softcover, 66pp.

BEGINNER'S GUIDE TO OBSERVING AND COLLECTING INSECTS. Here is the detailed information and practical tips needed by beginning and novice entomologists wanting to study the fascinating world of insects. Written in easy to understand language and filled with lots of illustrations, this guide covers topics such as what is an insect, insect growth and development, preparation for observing and collecting insects, where, when and how to look for insects, making an insect collection, interacting with other insect enthusiasts, and careers and scholarships. There is also an extensive bibliography and information on entomology resources. Softcover, 96pp.

For current information on availability and prices for any of these special publications, please contact the Young Entomologists' Society, Dept. PB, 1915 Peggy Place, Lansing, MI 48910-2553, tel. 517-887-0499.